JUDAISM:
A Dictionary

Arye Forta

Stanley Thornes (Publishers) Ltd

I wish to acknowledge the help given by Rev Michael Binstock, Senior Education Officer, Agency for Jewish Education and Rabbi Philip Ginsbury MA, Minister of South London Synagogue, who checked the entire manuscript. I thank them for their freely given time; any errors that escaped their eagle-eyed scrutiny are mine alone.

Text © Arye Forta, 1996

Original line illustrations © Stanley Thornes (Publishers) Ltd 1996

Illustrations by Kathy Baxendale, Celia Hart

The right of Arye Forta to be identified as author of this work has been asserted by him in accordance with the Copyright, Designs and Patents Act 1988.

First published in 1996 by:
Stanley Thornes (Publishers) Ltd
Ellenborough House
Wellington Street
CHELTENHAM GL50 1YW
England

96 97 98 99 00 / 10 9 8 7 6 5 4 3 2 1

A catalogue record for this book is available from the British Library.

ISBN 0 7487 2506 7

Typeset by Tech-Set, Gateshead
Printed and bound in Great Britain by
Redwood Books, Trowbridge, Wiltshire

GUIDE TO USING THE DICTIONARY

Introduction

This short dictionary is designed to help you understand the key terms, and to know something about the people, places and events, you will need for the Judaism component of the GCSE examination.

Signposts

None of these terms can really be taken in isolation; we understand things best when we see them in context. To help you do this, certain words appear in bold type. These words are signposts directing you to look elsewhere in the dictionary. For example, if you look up **shivah**, you will find a description of the Jewish week of mourning. But you will understand it much better if you look up the other words highlighted there, because then you will be able to place shivah in the context of other mourning customs. Similarly, if you want to find out about Theodor Herzl, the founder of the Zionist Movement, you will understand his life and work more fully by referring to the people and organisations that were connected with him.

Pronunciation

Many of the words in this dictionary are in Hebrew, the principal language of the Jewish scriptures and of Jewish prayer. Try to learn the correct pronunciation of these terms. There are two main ways of pronouncing Hebrew, the Sephardi (eastern) way and the Ashkenazi (western) style. The Sephardi has been used here, firstly because that is the way Hebrew is pronounced in modern Israel, where it is the spoken language, and secondly because many Jews, in particular young people, now use that pronunciation in prayer. However, if you should hear someone pronouncing it differently they may not be wrong – they are simply using the other method.

The pronunciation guide (set out in *italics*) is simple to follow; just stress the part of the word that appears in heavy type. Please remember that where the syllable *oo* appears in the pronunciation guide, it means a short sound, as in foot (not the long sound, as in food).

Plurals

Sometimes, the dictionary gives plural forms. These will make sense if you remember that all Hebrew nouns are either masculine or feminine (as in French). Feminine singular nouns often end with ah; feminine plural nouns end with ot. For example, on page 64, you will find that a **commandment** is mitzvah (feminine singular noun) and that commandments are mitzvot (feminine plural). There are no special endings for masculine singular nouns, but masculine plural nouns usually end with im. For example, on page 19, **cohen** is a priest, but priests are cohanim.

Het and chaf

Hebrew also has some sounds that do not exist in English, in particular the letters Het and Chaf. The former really sounds like a hoarse h, the latter rather like the ch in the Scottish loch or the Welsh bach. Sephardi Jews make a clear distinction between these sounds, whereas Ashkenazi Jews tend to pronounce them both as ch. Curiously, although many Jews in the west use the Sephardi pronunciation, they pronounce these letters as though they are the same, Ashkenazi style.

Unfortunately, text books differ in the way they represent these words in English. The Hebrew word for the bread Jews eat during Passover might be hametz in one book but chametz in another; and the Hebrew Bible might be referred to as Tenach or Tenakh. This is because Hebrew has a different alphabet and when we write Hebrew words in English letters we can usually only give an approximation. That is why, in some cases, this dictionary gives more than one version of the same word.

Maps

You will find these at the back of the dictionary.

A

Aaron Hebrew Aharon (*a-ha-ron*) Moses' older brother (Exodus 4:14). In Egypt, Aaron was Moses' spokesman in trying to persuade **Pharaoh** to release the Israelite slaves. Later, Aaron, together with his sons, became the first Jewish **priests** (Exodus 28:1) and, from that time on, priesthood was passed on to Aaron's descendants. Aaron died on Mount Hor, within sight of the **Promised Land**. In Jewish tradition, Aaron is remembered as the great peacemaker. **Hillel**, a famous first century teacher, said, 'Be of the followers of Aaron, loving peace, pursuing peace, loving people and bringing them close to the **Torah**.' ▶ See **cohen**.

Abraham Hebrew Avraham (*av-ra-ham*) the father of the Jewish people. Abram (as he was originally called) was born about 38 centuries ago in Ur, a major centre of moon worship (now in southern Iraq). With his father, he migrated to Haran (now in northern Syria). There, at the age of 75, God called him to uproot himself and go to a new land (Genesis 12:1–5). In Jewish tradition, this call came after many years of searching for the one, true God. When Abram reached **Canaan** (now called **Israel**) God promised him, 'I will give this land to your descendants' (verse 7).

Later, God changed Abram's name to Abraham, meaning 'father of many nations'. He told Abraham to circumcise himself and his son as a sign of their **covenant**, bond, with God (Genesis, chapter 17). According to tradition, Abraham was in the habit of praying in the early morning and so instituted the idea of **shacharit**, the morning service. ▶ See also **milah**, **patriarchs**.

Adar the 12th month of the Jewish year. Adar 13th is the **Fast of Esther** and the following day is **Purim**. During a leap year (which occurs 7 times in every cycle of 19 years) there are two Adars, Adar Rishon, the first Adar and Adar Sheni, the second. When this occurs, the Fast of Esther and Purim are celebrated in the second Adar.

Afikomen (*a-fee-ko-man*) Greek, dessert. A piece of matzah (unleavened bread) taken to symbolise the **Passover** sacrifice Jews used to eat when the **Temple** stood. At the beginning of the **seder**, the Passover meal, part of a matzah is put aside to be eaten as afikomen at the end. ▶ See also **korban pesach**.

Aggadah (*a-ga-dah*) lit. telling, the narrative sections of the **Talmud** or **Midrash**. The stories, which might be taken from real life or built around well-known people, were generally used for teaching moral or spiritual values. Jews sometimes use the **Aramaic** term aggadeta.

Agudat Yisrael (*a-gu-dat yis-ra-el*) 'Union of Israel', an organisation formed in 1912 to counter the expanding influence of the **Reform** and **Zionist** movements and preserve the **Orthodox** way of life in the face of increasing **secularism** and **assimilation**. It rapidly became an international movement with branches in many countries and developed a women's movement (Neshei Agudat Yisrael) and a youth movement (Zeirei Agudat Yisrael). The movement was politically active, opposing co-operation with **secularised** Zionists and working to uphold the **halakhah**, Jewish law, as the ultimate authority in Jewish society. However, when the **Nazis** came to power, Agudat Yisrael did work together with the **Zionists** to rescue Jews from Germany. Since the establishment of the State of Israel, the movement has campaigned for the Jewish State to be run along **Torah** lines.

Agunah (*a-gu-nah*) a woman bound to her husband. Originally, agunah meant a woman whose husband was missing but not known to be dead. Today it may also refer to a woman whose husband refuses to give her a divorce. Either way, she is 'bound' to him in that she is not free to remarry.

Ahad Ha'am lit. 'one of the people', pen name of Asher Ginsberg (1856–1927), one of the most influential of the early Zionist thinkers. Unlike **Herzl**, whose **Zionism** was solely political (ie aimed at creating a Jewish homeland), Ginsberg saw **Palestine** as the future Jewish cultural centre where, once Jews were settled on its soil, Jewish art, music and literature would flourish. At the same time, he warned that unless Jews understood the needs of the existing Arab community in Palestine, they would trigger off tensions unwittingly. Ginsberg believed in the revival of Hebrew as a national language (▶ see **Ben Yehudah**) and opposed the **Reform Movement** in principle, believing that changes in **halakhah**, Jewish law, would come about as a matter of course rather than by deliberate reform. ▶ See also **Mohilever**.

Akedah lit. binding, always used to mean the binding of Isaac, when God told **Abraham** to offer his only son as a sacrifice (Genesis 22:2). After Isaac was bound and placed on the altar, an angel appeared and told Abraham, 'Do not stretch out your hand against the boy…now I know that you fear God and that you would not have withheld your only son from me' (verse 12). In Jewish tradition, this was the last of Abraham's ten trials.

Akiva, Rabbi (d.135 CE) also spelt Akiba. An untutored man in his early years, he began studying at the age of 40 and became one of the leading scholars of the pre-Mishnaic period. He continued the work of Hillel, ordering the vast body of halakhic rulings, Jewish law, into a system. This paved the way for further classification that led to the **Mishnah**. Rabbi Akiva taught that since the **Torah** was revealed by God, every word, letter and unusual spelling has a purpose. He demonstrated this by relating particular halakhot, laws, to the wording of the Torah. Rabbi Akiva supported **Bar Kokhba's** revolt in 132 CE. After the revolt collapsed, he was tortured and killed by the Romans.

Alenu (*a-le-nu*) a prayer said at the end of each of the three daily services. The name is taken from the opening words *alenu leshabe'ach laadon hakol*, 'It is our duty to praise the Master of all things'. Alenu consists of two paragraphs. The first reflects upon the Jews' special duties towards God; the second looks forward to a future time when all people on earth will recognise and worship the one, true God.

Aliyah (*a-li-yah*) lit. ascent,
1) being called to recite a blessing over the reading of the **Torah**, so called because one ascends the **bimah**, platform, where the Torah scroll is read and also because the opportunity to recite the blessing is a spiritual elevation. **2)** settling in **Israel**, so called because Jews believe Israel to be under special divine care (cf. Deuteronomy 11:12) and

therefore holier than any other place on earth.

Almemar (*al-may-mar*) also spelt almemor, from the Arabic *alminbar*, pulpit (of the mosque). ▶ See **bimah**.

Amah (*a-mah*) the standard Biblical measure of length, roughly equivalent to the distance from a man's elbow to the tip of his middle finger. At the time of the second temple, it was reckoned to be exactly 18 inches.

Amen (*ah-men*) lit. it is so, it is correct, response to hearing a blessing or praise of God, acknowledging it to be true.

Amidah (*a-mi-dah*) lit. standing, another name for the **shemoneh esrei**, the 18 blessings that form the main part of the three daily prayers; so called because it is said standing, without leaning on anything (unless one is old or infirm). ▶ See also **tefillah**.

Amora (*a-mor-ra*) lit. speaker, plural amoraim; the Palestinian and Babylonian rabbis whose discussions formed the basis for the **Talmud**. Their main work was interpreting the teaching of the **Tannaim**, the rabbis responsible for the **Mishnah**. The amoraim flourished from the late 2nd to the 5th centuries CE.

Amos (Hebrew *a-mos*) a prophet of the mid 8th century BCE, a farmer from Judah whom God called to prophecy in **Israel**. Amos attacked the materialism of the wealthy classes, their dishonest gain, love of luxury and callous oppression of the poor. An official of the idolatrous temple of Bethel tried to prevent him from speaking. He taught that unless Israel repented, the nation would be lost.

Amos, book of third book of **Trei Asar**, the Twelve Prophets. The book is structured in four parts; (i) chapters 1:1–2:6, prophecies against the nations surrounding Israel, (ii) chapters 2:7–6:14, prophecies against the sinful Israelites, (iii) chapters 7:1–9:6, events in Amos' own life, (iv) chapter 9:7 to the end, prophecies of comfort for the Jewish people.

Anthropomorphism Greek *anthropos* (man) and *morphe* (shape), ie speaking of God as though He has a human form. Although Judaism has always taught that God cannot be visualised, the **Torah** often uses anthropomorphisms. These are of two types; those wherein God is referred to as possessing human limbs and organs, eg God's feet (Exodus 24:10) or God's eyes (Deuteronomy 11:12) and those where God is described as performing human actions such as speaking (Genesis 1:3) or seeing (verse 4). The purpose of anthropomorphisms is to make God's actions accessible to human understanding.

Antiochus a Greek king who ruled the Syrian Empire from 175–164 BCE. From the time Antiochus ascended the throne, he found himself in desperate need of money to pay off a massive debt his father owed to Rome. A group of hellenised Jews (ie Jews who had adopted Greek ways) offered him a large sum in return for him installing them as rulers of Jerusalem. Antiochus agreed. However, they could not raise the sum and resorted to plundering the Temple. This provoked a riot which Antiochus crushed with armed police. Seeing Judaism as the cause of the people's unrest, he passed a series of decrees with the intention of abolishing it. This triggered off the **Maccabean Revolt**. ▶ See also **Hanukah**.

Anti-semitism dislike or hatred of Jews. Anti-semitism has taken many forms – Jews have been disliked for being too rich and for being too poor; for being communists and for being capitalists; for being uncultured and for being too sophisticated. **Nazi** propaganda portrayed Jews as a sub-human species. Various reasons have been suggested for anti-semitism, none of them entirely satisfactory. Much present day anti-semitism probably has its roots in religion – in the Christian belief that Jesus is God and that the Jews killed him and the Muslim belief that Muhammad was God's final prophet whom the Jews rejected. ▶ See **Autoemancipation, final solution, pogrom, Shoah.**

Apocrypha Greek for 'hidden things', a collection of writings not included in the **Tenakh**, the Jewish Bible; called in Hebrew *sefarim hitzoniim*, books left out [of the Torah], ie hidden away. The books of the Apocrypha are: I and II Esdras, Tobit, Judith, Additions to Esther, The Wisdom of Solomon, Ecclesiasticus, Baruch, The Letter of Jeremiah, The Song of the Three Men, Susanna, Bel and the Dragon, The Prayer of Menasseh, I and II Maccabees. Among this collection are historical writings, books giving moral guidance and prayers, fictional stories with moral or spiritual themes and others that describe people's visions. All these books were written between about 200 BCE and 100 CE. Jews do not regard them as sacred.

Aramaic a language related to **Hebrew**. Some parts of the **Tenakh**, the Jewish Bible are in Aramaic, in particular Genesis 31:47, Jeremiah 10:11 and parts of the books of **Ezra** and **Daniel**. It was the Jews' main spoken language during the first five centuries CE and several translations of the **Torah** were made into it. It is also the language of the two **Talmuds**. Some prayers composed in Aramaic are still in use, most notably the **kaddish**, one form of which is the prayer said by mourners. ▶ See also **Targum**.

Aravot (*A-ra-vot*) plural of aravah, willow. Two sprigs of willow make up part of the **arbaat haminim**, the four plant species Jews use in

prayer during **Sukkot**, the festival of Tabernacles.

Arbaah Turim (*ar-ba-ah tu-rim*) lit. four rows, a code of Jewish law compiled by Rabbi Yaakov ben Asher (1270–1340), often called the Tur for short. It was the first code to omit the laws that had ceased to be observed after the destruction of the **Temple** (eg those relating to sacrifices). Rabbi Yaakov divided his work into four sections, **Orach Chayim** (the path of life), **Yoreh Deah** (teaching knowledge), **Even Haezer** (the rock of sustenance) and **Choshen Mishpat** (the breastplate of justice). In each section he set down the major rabbinic opinions up to his own time. The Arbaah Turim became the forerunner of the **Shulchan Aruch**, the most definitive code of Jewish law. ▶ See also **codes, responsa**.

Arba'at haminim (*ar-ba-at ha-mi-nim*) the four kinds ie the four plant species used during prayers on **Sukkot** (Tabernacles) – palm branch, citron, myrtle and willow (Leviticus 23:40). The two sprigs of willow and three of myrtle are tied (before the festival) to the palm branch. During **Hallel** (thanksgiving psalms) these four plants are held together and, at certain points in the prayer, are moved from all six directions (right, left, front, up, down and back) towards the worshipper's heart, symbolising the flow of God's blessings. Sukkot·occurs at the start of the rainy season in Israel and the morning service concludes with hoshanot, a ceremony that includes a prayer for rain. The four plants, all of which require an abundance of water, are also held during this prayer. ▶ See also **aravot, etrog, hadassim, lulav.**

Aron hakodesh – a golden box containing the **Ten Commandments**.

The four plants (**arba'at haminim**) used during prayers on **Sukkot**.

Ark see next entry.

Aron Hakodesh lit. holy ark. **1)** a golden box in the **Temple**, containing a close fitting wooden box with yet another golden box inside that. In it were the blocks of stone containing the **Ten Commandments** that **Moses** brought down from **Mount Sinai**, as well as other sacred objects. It was kept in the **Holy of Holies; 2)** the alcove or cupboard at the front of a **synagogue** in which the **Torah scrolls** are kept. It is normally covered with a curtain or screen. The ark is only opened to remove or return a scroll. It is also opened during certain prayers.

Arvit (*ar-vit*) the evening service, the first of the three daily prayers (since, in Jewish reckoning, the day begins at sunset). Also called maariv. It is said any time between sunset and midnight, this being the time when, at the end of the day's sacrifices in the **Temple**, the offerings would be left on the altar to smoulder. The Arvit service comprises two blessings, followed by **Shema** (the declaration of God's oneness), a further two or three blessings (customs vary) and the **amidah**, the standing prayer and **Aleinu**, the concluding prayer. The service normally takes between 10–15 minutes. Arvit for Sabbaths (Friday nights) is longer as it includes additional **Psalms**. ▶ See also **minchah, shacharit.**

Asarah b'Tevet (*a-sa-ra be-te-vet*), the tenth day of the month of Tevet, which occurs around November– December. It is one of the four fasts connected with the destruction of the **Temple** and the exile of the

Jewish people. Asarah b'Tevet marks the day the Babylonian army began the siege of Jerusalem in 586 BCE. ▶ See also **Shivah asar b' Tammuz, Tishah b'Av, Tzom Gedaliah.**

Aseret yemei teshuvah (*a-se-ret ye-mei te-shu-vah*) lit. ten days of returning (sometimes called the ten days of penitence); the ten days from **Rosh Hashanah**, the New Year, until **Yom Kippur**, the Day of Atonement. It is a time when Jews reflect on their relationship with God and try to make amends for the things they have done wrong. ▶ See also **teshuvah**.

Ashkenazim (*ash-ke-na-zim*) a term that originally meant German Jews, due to the fact that country had one of the first sizeable Jewish communities in Europe. With the migration of Jews to other parts of Europe (except Spain, see **Sephardim**), the term Ashkenazim now refers to European-type Jews anywhere (ie even in America and Australia).

Assimilation the desire to become part of, and indistinguishable from, the surrounding culture. When Jews assimilate, they usually start by shedding those observances that mark them out as different, eg, eating kosher food, and eventually casting off other practices too. Some Jews have seen assimilation as a means of avoiding **anti-semitism**, though this has seldom worked in

practice. ▶ See also **final solution, Herzl, Pinsker.**

Athalta digeulta (*at-hal-ta di-ge-ul-ta*) Aramaic, the beginning of the messianic redemption. ▶ See also **Kook, Mashiach.**

Auschwitz the largest Nazi concentration and extermination camp. From the time the **Nazis** launched their **Final Solution** in September 1941 until the camp was liberated by the Soviet Army in January 1945, over 1,000,000 Jews as well as gypsies, Russians and others, were murdered there. The name Auschwitz, more than that of any other concentration camp, has become a virtual symbol of the Holocaust. ▶ See also **Shoah** and map 4.

Autoemancipation a book published by Dr. Leon **Pinsker** in 1882 setting out the need for a Jewish homeland. As the name suggests, *Autoemancipation* was a call for Jews to free themselves from **anti-semitism** and persecution. Pinsker believed that the reasons for anti-semitism were social (Jews were a separate ethnic group which the other nations could neither accept nor absorb) and economic (the nations resented business competition from aliens). Pinsker argued that these problems would disappear if Jews had their own country.

Av the fifth month of the Jewish year (starting from Nisan). The first third

of the month is a period of
mourning. It ends after **Tishah b'Av**,
a fast that marks the destruction of
both **Temples** as well as other
tragedies. For this reason the month
is also called Menachem Av, the
comfort of Av, referring to the future
messianic age when Av is expected
to be a time of great joy. The 15th is a
semi festive day. It commemorates
the time, during the 11th century
BCE, following a civil war in which
one of the Israelite tribes was almost
wiped out. The other tribes took
pity on them and set aside the 15th
day of Av as a time when they
could choose brides from any tribe.

Avel (*a-vel*) a mourner, plural
avelim (*a-ve-lim*). When someone
dies, the immediate relations –
spouse, children, parents, brother
and sister – become avelim. For
details, see next word.

Avelut (*a-ve-lut*) mourning.
Mourning in Judaism has two
functions; it creates opportunities for
bereaved people to grieve but is
structured to help them phase out
their grief. Avelut does not begin till
after the funeral, since mourners are
expected to be occupied with caring
for the body and arranging the
burial. After the funeral comes the
shivah – a seven day period of
intense mourning. This is followed

by the **sheloshim**, a period of
three more weeks during which time
the mourners start resuming normal
life again, although they still keep
some mourning laws. Avelut for
parents lasts for an entire year.
▶ See also **chevra kaddisha, kaddish
yatom, onen,** and **yarzheit.**

Avodah zarah (*a-vo-dah za-rah*)
lit. alien worship – the worship of
anything other than God. Avodah
zarah includes the worship of the
sun or moon, animals or plants, a
person or a process (eg fire). In
Jewish teaching, these are forbidden
to Jews and non-Jews alike. The
name 'alien worship' reflects the
Jewish belief that all people are
creatures of God and that any other
worship is, therefore, alien to a
person's true nature.

Avot lit. fathers; **1)** the ancestors of
the Jewish people (see **Patriarchs**),
2) an abridged name for **Pirkei Avot**,
a volume of the **Mishnah** that offers
moral guidance.

Avraham avinu (*av-ra-ham
a-vee-noo*) our father **Abraham**, a
term of reverence and endearment
Jews use recognising Abraham
as their first ancestor. ▶ See
Patriarchs.

Baal Shem Tov, Rabbi Yisrael

(1698–1760) lit. master of the good name, ie the name of God; the founder of the **Hasidic Movement**. Rabbi Yisrael lived at a time when wars, persecution and an epidemic had reduced the once vibrant Jewish communities of Poland to a fraction of their former size. In addition, the **Torah** scholars, in particular in nearby Lithuania, tended to look down on their unlearned Polish brethren as second class Jews. Rabbi Yisrael set out to address the widespread dejection that was all around him. Originally, he had associated with the **nistarim**, the concealed mystics. However, around 1734, he realised that their work was inadequate for the task in hand. He felt that the time had come to reveal those parts of the **kabbalah**, Jewish mysticism, that had formerly been studied only by a select few, and began teaching them publicly. He taught that the ultimate purpose of serving God is **devekut**, attachment to Him (ie a feeling of oneness with the divine) and that even unlearned Jews could accomplish this if they prayed and observed the commandments with enthusiasm, devotion and joy. He insisted that true Torah study was not a cold, analytical exercise of the mind alone but a deep personal attachment to God's will and wisdom. Although Rabbi Yisrael's teachings had immediate appeal to the unlearned masses, a number of Torah scholars also appreciated his approach and devoted themselves to mastering the path he pointed out. These scholars provided the future leadership of the movement he started. ▶ See also **hasidut, kavannah**.

Babylon

Hebrew Bavel (*ba-vel*), roughly the same area as modern Iraq. The Jewish community of Babylon began in the early 6th century BCE, when thousands of Jews were deported there. The main areas of Jewish settlement were along the banks of the Euphrates where they flourished for well over a thousand years. For much of the time, the Jews had their own rulers (▶ see **exilarch**) and, sometimes, even their own armies that helped the local princes in their wars with the Romans. There, Jewish scholars produced the **Talmud Bavli**, Babylonian Talmud, still studied as the basis for all **halakhah**, Jewish law. ▶ See map 2.

Babylonian exile

the Jews were exiled to Babylon in three waves. In 597 BCE, the upper classes and skilled workers were taken. After the destruction of Jerusalem in 586 BCE, the rest of the population was deported, leaving a small group behind under Gedaliah ben Ahikam. When he was assassinated (▶ see **Tzom Gedaliah**), some Jews fled to Egypt and those who remained were taken to Babylon. The exile created a major crisis of faith. Some Jews questioned God's justice, complaining that their fathers had sinned and that they were being punished; others felt that the loss of the Temple meant the end of Judaism. It was mainly the prophet **Ezekiel**, deported with the first wave, and **Jeremiah** who kept in contact from Jerusalem, who steered the exiles through the crises and kept Judaism alive.

Baeck, Leo (1873–1956), **Reform** minister and theologian. Baeck served Reform congregations in Germany before World War II. When the Nazis came to power, he was offered opportunities to escape but refused, preferring to work to conserve the Jews' dwindling civic rights. In 1943 he was sent to Theresienstadt concentration camp, where he tried to keep some form of Jewish spirit alive. Baeck believed that God had not given the **Torah** at Mount Sinai, maintaining instead that every now and then God's will breaks through to people in sudden flashes of insight. For Baeck, the most important aspect of Judaism was its ethical teaching (compare **ethical monotheism**). He taught that ritual was only of value when it led to ethical awareness.

Balfour Declaration a letter written by the British foreign secretary, James Arthur Balfour, to Lord Rothschild on November 2nd 1917. In it, he writes 'His Majesty's Government views with favour the establishment in Palestine of a national home for the Jewish people, and will use their best endeavour to facilitate the achievement of this objective, it being clearly understood that nothing shall be done which may prejudice the civil and religious rights of existing non-Jewish communities in Palestine, or the rights and political status enjoyed by Jews in any other country.' He concludes by asking Lord Rothschild to 'bring this declaration to the knowledge of the Zionist Federation'.

Bar Kokhba (*bar kokh-ba*) lit. son of a star, a title of honour given to Simon bar Kosiba who, in 132 CE, led a rebellion against the Roman forces in Judea. He drove them out of Jerusalem and, with the support of Rabbi **Akiva**, set up his own independent government. In 135 CE, his army was defeated in the battle of Betar where he was killed.

Bar mitzvah (*bar mitz-vah*) lit. son of the commandments, ie a boy who, at the age of 13, reaches Jewish adulthood and becomes responsible to observe the commandments of the **Torah**. Through usage, the term has also come to mean the ceremony that marks the occasion, However, a boy becomes bar mitzvah (ie an adult and responsible) regardless of whether he has a ceremony or not.

Baruch shepatarani (*ba-ruch she-pa-ta-ra-ni*) a short blessing said by the father of a child becoming an adult, thanking God for having brought the child to an age when they can take responsibility for their own actions.

Bat chayil (*bat-cha-yil*) lit. daughter of worth, a ceremony that girls choose to take part in to mark their entry into Jewish womanhood. It takes place in the synagogue any time after a girl's 12th birthday, usually on a Sunday. Sometimes two or more girls celebrate together. A girl prepares by studying various aspects of Jewish womanhood and, on the day, usually gives a speech.

Bat mitzvah (*bat-mitz-vah*) lit. daughter of the commandments, ie a girl who, at the age of 12, becomes responsible to observe the commandments of the Torah. In the past, there was no ceremony to mark a girl's bat mitzvah. Today, bat mitzvah celebrations are becoming common.

Becher (*be-cher*) Yiddish cup or goblet (compare English beaker), a name **Ashkenazi** Jews give to the silver wine cup used for **kiddush**, the blessing of sanctification, said at the beginning of Sabbath or festive meals. Called *kos* in Hebrew.

Bedikat hametz (*be-dee-kat cha-metz*) the search for leaven. On

Passover, Jews are not permitted to eat leaven, ie grain products that have risen due to the action of yeasts. During the days before Passover, they clean their houses to remove all trace of leaven. On the night before Passover, they search the house with a candle and feather (the ancient equivalent of the torch and brush). Traditionally, ten pieces of bread are laid out for the searchers to find. The reason for this is **kabbalistic**; however, it acts as a check that the search has been carried out properly.

Bemidbar (*be-mid-bar*) the fourth book of the **Tenakh**, the Jewish Bible; called **Numbers** in English. Bemidbar starts with a census of the Israelites, then goes on to describe a rebellion against Moses' leadership, attempts by hostile tribes to defeat the Israelites and the Israelites' conquests east of the Jordan. It concludes with an outline of the route they had taken from Egypt to the borders of the **Promised Land**. ▶ See also **Moses**.

Ben Gurion, David (1886-1973) **Zionist** leader and first Prime Minister of modern Israel. Born in Poland to a Zionist family, Ben Gurion settled in **Palestine** at the age of 20. He soon became a leading Zionist speaker, insisting on the use of **Hebrew**, as opposed to **Yiddish** (which he regarded as *sefat hagalut*, the language of exile). He insisted that the Jewish settlers of Palestine run their own affairs without any interference from the **Diaspora**, and

organised the workers into a movement for economic improvement and political change. After World War II, Ben Gurion encouraged 'illegal' immigration and political opposition to British control, and helped organise a Jewish army to resist the forthcoming Arab attack. Once the State of Israel was established in 1948, he dismissed the Diaspora history – a period of nearly 2000 years – as though it never happened. For him, the new Jewish state was a continuation of the one destroyed by the Romans in 70 CE.
▶ See also **Mandate**.

Ben Yehudah, Eliezer

(1858–1922) the father of modern Hebrew. The Russo-Turkish war (1877–78), when the Balkan people struggled for independence, inspired him with the ideal of an independent Jewish homeland with its national language. From the time he arrived in **Palestine** in 1886, he and his wife spoke only Hebrew in their home. Ben Yehudah quickly fell out with religious Jews for whom Hebrew was a sacred tongue (see **leshon hakodesh**), whereas he regarded it as the secular language of Jewish nationalism. He adopted the **Sephardi** pronunciation of Hebrew. In 1910, he began work on a *Complete Dictionary of Ancient and Modern Hebrew* (though it was not completed till 40 years after his death). He struggled to make Hebrew the everyday language of the Jews in Palestine, and developed new words to meet the needs of modern life.

Berachah (*be-ra-chah*) lit. blessing, plural berachot (*be-ra-chot*); a prayer or statement beginning or ending with the words 'Blessed are you God'. There are three types of berachah; (i) blessings praising God, these form part of the daily prayers, (ii) blessings recited before performing a **mitzvah**, religious obligation (eg before reading from a Torah scroll), (iii) blessings said before and after eating or drinking, to thank God for providing human needs.

Bereshit (*be-re-shit*) the first book of the **Tenakh**, the Jewish Bible; called **Genesis** in English. Bereshit opens with an account of how God created the world. It describes how people became wicked, how God destroyed them with a flood and spared Noah and his family to start human life anew. It tells of the lives of the Patriarchs and Matriarchs, the ancestors of the Jewish people and ends with the career of **Joseph** and how **Jacob** and his family settled in Egypt.

Bet din (*bet din*) lit. house of justice, a rabbinic court. A bet din has neither jury nor defending and prosecuting counsels. The judges themselves question the witnesses and give their verdict. There is always an odd number of judges and never less than three. Today, rabbinic courts do not try criminal cases. They are used by Jews who go to arbitration with other Jews (eg, business disputes) and want their case judged according to Jewish law.

They also preside over conversions to Judaism and are responsible for supervising caterers and other individuals involved in the production of kosher food.

Bet din hagadol (*bet din* ha-ga-*dol*) lit. great house of justice, the supreme rabbinical court, also called the **Sanhedrin**. This was a court of 71 judges which, in ancient times, sat in the Chamber of Hewn Stones, one of the halls in the **Temple**. Its power was restricted by the Roman authorities some years before the second Temple was destroyed though it continued to perform important religious functions long after the destruction.

Bet haknesset (*bet hak-ness-et*) lit. house of assembly, a **synagogue**. ('Synagogue' is Greek translation of bet haknesset.) The name reflects the fact that synagogues are community centres, ie places where people gather for communal events, not just places of worship.

Bet hamidrash (*bet ha-mid-rash*) lit. house of study, a synagogue whose main function is **Torah** study rather than prayer. Every **yeshivah** and **kollel** (Jewish academy) has a bet hamidrash for its students; some synagogues have a small bet hamidrash for use of the Jewish public.

Bet hamikdash (*bet ha-mik-dash*) lit. house of sanctity, the **Temple**, plural batei mikdash. The first bet hamikdash was built by King

Solomon in the late 10th century BCE, on the model of the **mishkan**, the portable temple the Israelites constructed in the desert. It was destroyed by the Babylonians in 586 BCE. A second bet hamikdash was built by the Jews who returned from **Babylonian exile**; it was destroyed by the Romans in 70 CE.

Bet Yaakov (*bet Ya-a-kov*) lit. house of Jacob; a movement for Jewish girls' education started by Sarah **Scheneirer** in the early years of this century.

Betzah (*be-tzah*) egg; an egg, usually roasted, is placed on the **seder plate** at the Passover meal. It calls to mind the festival sacrifice that used to be offered in the Temple on the **shalosh regalim**, the three pilgrim festivals (**Pesach, Shavuot,** and **Sukkot**).

Bimah (*bee-mah*) a raised platform in the **synagogue** from where the **Torah** is read. It is modelled on the platform which Ezra set up in the **Temple** (see **Ezra**). In some synagogues, the person leading the service may stand there. Communal announcements are also made from the bimah. ► See **almemar**.

Birkat erusin (*bir-kat e-roo-sin*) blessing recited at the beginning of a wedding ceremony. In it, the person conducting the wedding thanks God for sanctifying the Jewish people through the **Torah's** marriage laws. ► See also **erusin, nisuin, shevah brachot**.

Birkat cohanim (*bir-kat co-ha-nim*) the blessing given by the priests, ie God's blessing conveyed to the congregation by the priests; a recitation of Numbers 6:24–26. In Israel, the priests perform this ceremony every day; everywhere else in the world, they do so only on festivals. On other days, it is read during the repetition of the amidah, the standing prayer, in the morning and additional services. ▶ See also **Cohen**.

Birkot nisuin (*bir-chot nis-oo-in*) blessings recited at the conclusion of a marriage ceremony. There are seven blessings, praising God for creating humanity, and granting happiness to the bride and groom ▶ See also **erusin, nisuin**.

Bitter herbs ▶ see **maror**.

Blech Yiddish for tin, a sheet of metal. Jews are not permitted to cook on the Sabbath, so food is prepared beforehand and left on the cooker. Placing a blech over the cooker top ensures that the controls are covered and will not be touched. It also makes it possible to position a saucepan where the food will remain hot overnight without burning to a cinder.

Blood libel accusations against Jews claiming that they killed Christian children for their blood. The first recorded blood libel took place at Norwich during the Easter of 1144, when a local child went missing. The Jews were accused of crucifying him to mock the crucifixion of Jesus. Subsequently, Easter (preceded by Good Friday which, in the Christian calender marks the crucifixion) became the standard time for such accusations. Later in the Middle Ages, Christians noted that Easter often coincided with **Passover** and the Jews were accused of using Christian blood to bake their **matzah** (unleavened bread). Blood libels were revived by the **Nazis** as part of their anti-Jewish propaganda.

Brit covenant, an agreement where two or more parties agree to abide by certain conditions for each other's benefit. Jews see their relationship with God as a covenant; Jews pledge themselves to keep the God's laws, God pledges Himself never to completely abandon the Jewish people. The word is also used to refer to circumcision (see next entry), the sign of the covenant.

Brit milah (*brit mee-lah*) lit. the covenant of circumcision, ie circumcision as a sign of the bond between the Jews and God, as laid down in Genesis 17: 9–12. It is carried out when a baby boy is eight days old (unless the child is not well) and is performed by a **mohel**, who acts on behalf of the child's father; the father having the obligation to circumcise his son. A Jew who reaches adulthood without brit milah is obligated to have himself circumcised. The circumcision of adults is usually carried out by a Jewish doctor qualified in the technique. Circumcision is also required for non-Jewish males wishing to become Jewish. ▶ See also **gerut**.

Buber, Martin (1878–1965) philosopher of religion and **Zionist** leader. Buber maintained that Zionism should be cultural rather than political and that the ideal Zionist state was a Jewish-Arab republic. His religious philosophy was greatly influenced by **Hasidut**, Hasidic thought (which **Hasidim** themselves maintain he failed to understand). His best known contribution was his book I*ch und Du* (*I and Thou*), published in 1923. In it, he distinguishes between an I–thou and an I–it relationship. The former is a direct relationship, an experience of intense closeness with a person or object (which Buber called **dialogue**); the second is a relationship that allows one to stand back and analyse that person or object in a detached way. Buber saw our relationships with God, people and the world constantly interchanging between these two forms. Buber has had little impact on Jewish thought, though he has influenced some Christian theologians.

Bund a Jewish socialist movement active in Russia during the 19th century. The Bund campaigned to have Jews officially recognised as one of the national groups that made up the Russian Empire with their own territory in the **Pale of Settlement**. They cultivated **Yiddish** as their national language as opposed to the **Hebrew** of the **Zionists**. ▶ See map 3.

C

Canaan the land God promised the **Patriarchs**, the fathers of the Jewish people, would one day belong to their descendants; roughly corresponding to modern **Israel**. In the **Torah** it is called after the Canaanites, the principal people living there at the time of **Joshua's** conquest. ▶ See map 1.

Caro, Rabbi Joseph (1488–1575) the foremost **halakhic** authority of his day and author of the **Shulchan Aruch**. The Shulchan Aruch itself is a digest of Rabbi Caro's major work *Bet Yosef*, the 'House of Joseph', which he worked on for 20 years. He wrote *Bet Yosef* as a commentary on the **Arbaah Turim**, an earlier halakhic work, intending to bring order to the mass of halakhic rulings that had accumulated by his day and show how they had emerged from the **Talmud**. His Shulchan Aruch was published in 1565, and rapidly became the standard text book of **halakhah**.

Carpas (*car-pas*) a vegetable eaten at the **seder**, the Passover meal – usually radish, potato or parsley. Carpas is an anagram of the Hebrew perech, hard labour plus the Hebrew character for 60 (in Hebrew, all the letters of the alphabet represent numbers; see **gematria**). This symbolises the sixty myriads (groups of 10,000) who left Egypt. ▶ See also **Pesach**, **seder**.

Chag a festival, plural chagim (*cha-gim*); strictly speaking, the term chag refers to the major festivals, **Pesach**, **Shavuot**, **Sukkot** and **Shemini Atzeret**. However, people tend to use it for almost any festive celebration.

Chag sameach (*chag sa-me-ach*) lit. a joyous festival, a greeting and parting Jews use on a festival (compare **Shabbat Shalom**).

Chalaf (*cha-laf*) the knife used in **shechitah**, the Jewish method of animal slaughter. Judaism forbids causing unnecessary pain to an animal, so the chalaf has to be kept razor sharp (a cut with a very sharp blade is usually not felt; a blunt knife causes pain). After killing an animal, the slaughterer checks the chalaf. If he detects any loss of sharpness, he

will hone it before using it on the next animal. ▶ See also **shechitah**, **tsar baalei chayim**.

Challah (*cha-lah*) **1)** a tithe of dough given to the priests in ancient times. Today, challah is taken from doughs over a certain size and destroyed since it cannot be given to the priests. **2)** a loaf of bread, usually plaited; plural challot (*cha-lot*) . Two challot are put on the table at the beginning of Sabbath and festival meals (except Passover). They symbolise the double portion of manna, the food the Israelites ate in the desert (Exodus 16:14–16), that appeared each Sabbath eve.

Chametz ▶ see **hametz**.

Chamesh Megillot (*cha-mesh me-gi-lot*) the five scrolls, the Biblical books of **Song of Songs, Ruth, Ecclesiastes, Lamentations** and **Esther**; so called because unlike the other books of the prophets, where only small sections are read in public worship (▶ see **haftarah**), these books are read in their entirety. ▶ See individual entries for details.

Chamishah chumshei Torah (*cha-mi-shah chum-shei To-rah*) lit. five fifths of the **Torah**, printed books of the Torah that Jews have in their homes and use for study, rather than Torah scrolls which are much too costly for most people to afford. Usually called **chumash** for short.

Chanukah ▶ see **Hanukah**.

Chatan Bereshit (*cha-tan Be-re-shit*) lit. bridegroom of **Bereshit**, Genesis, the first part of the Torah; the person called to commence the new cycle of Torah readings on **Simchat Torah**.

Chatan Torah (*cha-tan To-rah*) lit. bridegroom of the **Torah**, the person called to the reading of the final portion of **Devarim**, Deuteronomy on **Simchat Torah**.

Chaver (*cha-ver*) companion, associate. **1)** A member of the Chavurah, an association that flourished during the first two centuries CE, whose members undertook to be particularly careful with separating tithes and maintaining a high standard of purity, **2)** A companion with whom one studies (▶ see next entry). Also spelt haver.

Chavruta (*chav-roo-ta*) **Aramaic**, companionship, a method of study developed in the **yeshivot**, Talmudic academies, whereby students work with a chaver, companion, ie study in pairs, reading, discussing and analysing the Talmud or other text together. In large yeshivot, over 100 pairs might be studying in the same way and students have to learn to block out all other voices and hear only their own chaver. Girls' **seminaries** also use the chavruta system.

Chazan (*cha-zan*) person who leads the prayers in the synagogue, plural chazanim (*cha-za-nim*) . Unlike the

sheliach tzibbur, who simply sets and maintains the pace at which prayers are said, the chazan chants them, providing musical renditions of certain key parts of the service. Sometimes a chazan will be helped by a choir. Chazanim also provide light musical entertainment at functions by singing Jewish songs.

Cheder (*che-der*) lit. room, originally a place of primary Jewish education as opposed to the **yeshivah**, a Jewish academy. Today, the term is used to refer to synagogue religion classes. ▶ See **Talmud Torah**.

Cheshvan eigth month of the Jewish year, roughly corresponding to November–December. There are no festivals in Cheshvan.

Chevra kaddisha (*chev-ra ka-dee-sha*) lit. Holy Society, the people who prepare bodies for burial by washing them and dressing them in linen shrouds. Men prepare male bodies; women prepare females. The name reflects the Jewish belief that the body is the earthly container for the soul and is therefore to be treated with dignity. Chevra kaddisha members are always volunteers – it is considered wrong to take payment for a holy task. ▶ See also **avelut, levayah, onen**.

Chevrat musar (*chav-rat mus-ar*) lit. ethics society, a society for the study of **musar**, Jewish religious ethics, founded by Rabbi Israel **Lipkin** of Salant in 1842. The chevrat musar published ethical works and tried to encourage businessmen to devote time during their day to studying them. The project failed and Rabbi Lipkin turned his attention to educating the youth.

Chief Rabbi not a supreme religious authority (eg like the Pope for Roman Catholics) but rather a rabbi designated as the main spokesman for the Jews in a particular country. In the Middle Ages, chief rabbis were similar to executive directors administrating Jewish communal life; sometimes they were responsible for collecting taxes from Jewish subjects. In England, the Chief Rabbinate originated in 1845, when the rabbi of London's Great Synagogue was appointed Chief Rabbi of the United Hebrew Congregations of the British Empire. In Israel there is a **Sephardi** Chief Rabbi (known as the Rishon Letzion) and an **Ashkenazi** Chief Rabbi. Both serve for a limited term.

Chok (*chok*) law, plural chukim (*choo-kim*), commandments in the **Torah** for which no reason is given. Examples of chukim are the command to eat only the meat of **kosher** animals (Leviticus chapter 11) or not to wear **shatnez**, mixtures of linen and wool in the same garment (Deuteronomy 22:11). Jews observe chukim as acts of faith.
▶ See also **edot, mishpatim**.

Chol hamoed (*chol ha-mo-ed*) lit. the ordinary (ie non sacred) days of the festival. Only the first and last days of **Passover** and **Sukkot** are actual holy days, the middle days are chol hamoed, when certain forms of work are permitted.

Choshen Mishpat (*cho-shen Mish-pat*) lit. the breastplate of justice, the fourth part of the **Arbaah Turim** and **Shulchan Aruch**, important **codes** of Jewish law. Choshen mishpat deals with civil law and includes the rules relating to judges and witnesses, damages, loans, documents and inheritance.

Chronicles, Book of Hebrew Divrei Hayamim (*div-rei ha-ya-mim*) 'Happenings of the times', last book of the **Ketuvim**, the holy writings and final book of the **Tenakh**, the Jewish Bible; it is a summary of the history of the Israelites until the **Babylonian exile**. The first nine chapters list the family trees of the Israelite tribes. Starting from chapter ten, Chronicles recounts the events of the reigns of **David, Solomon** and the other kings of **Judah**. Due to its size, later scholars divided the book into two parts, called First and Second Chronicles. According to the Talmud, it was written by **Ezra**.

Chumash (*chu-mash*) short for Chamishah Chumshei Torah, lit. the five parts (or fifths) of the **Torah**, plural chumashim (*chu-ma-shim*); a printed book containing the Five Books of Moses. Chumashim are used both for private study (since most Jews do not have **Torah scrolls** in their homes) and for following the Torah reading in the synagogue.

Chupah ▶ see **huppah**.

Circumcision ▶ see **milah**.

Codes digests of **halakhah**, Jewish law. Originally, codes were intended to help rabbis formulate their rulings, later they became instruments for helping students understand the **halakhah** as well as manuals for guiding the average Jew in his or her practice of Judaism. The earliest codes followed the order of the **Talmud**. **Maimonides' Mishneh Torah** was the first to break with the Talmudic structure, setting out the halakhot under subject headings. The **Arbaah Turim** of Rabbi Yaakov ben Asher used a simpler, four-part order, which was followed by the **Shulchan Aruch** and all subsequent codes. Modern codes tend to be books that concentrate on specific areas of halakhah, eg Sabbath, mourning customs.

Cohen (*co-hen*) a priest, plural cohanim (*co-ha-nim*) . Unlike **rabbis**, who may be drawn from any section of the Jewish community, only the descendants of **Aaron, Moses'** brother, are cohanim (though cohanim may also be rabbis). In the **Temple**, the cohanim used to handle the sacrifices. In the synagogue, they have no special function except to bless the congregation on certain occasions (▶ see **bircat cohanim**). A cohen is also called to the reading of the **Torah** before other Jews.

Confession ▶ see **vidui**.

Conservative Movement a movement that began in Germany with the moderate reforms of **Zacharias Frankel** but developed mainly in the United States. Originally, it stood for a traditional style Judaism wherein small changes were seen as necessary if Jews were to adapt to modern life. It stood in opposition to the **Reform Movement**, whose leaders, particularly in the U.S. where each congregation was independent of every other, were introducing far-reaching changes into their Judaism. Indeed, when, in 1885, the American Reform leaders voted to discontinue many Jewish practices, the conservatives voiced their opposition. However, by the 1930s, more radical men were moving into positions of influence within the Conservative Movement and a Reform-style trend began to emerge. In 1943, the conservatives began co-operating with the Reform Movement. Gradually, they abandoned the second day of the festivals, permitted their ministers to annul marriages when there were difficulties in obtaining a **get**, a Jewish divorce, and allowed certain kinds of work on the **Sabbath** day.

Continual light ▶ see **ner tamid**.

Conversion ▶ see **gerut**.

Covenant ▶ see **brit**.

Cubit ▶ see **amah**.

Daniel a pious Jew who rose to prominence in the court of Nebuchadnezzar, king of **Babylon** (604–562 BCE). He was renowned for his wisdom and the king consulted him on the meaning of dreams. Daniel observed his religion secretly, especially after Nebuchadnezzar issued a decree that everyone must worship him. Daniel's enemies informed Nebuchadnezzar, who ordered him to be thrown into a lions' den with a huge stone placed over the entrance. The following morning, when the king came to see Daniel's remains, he found him sitting calmly among the lions. Daniel was released and his enemies were thrown in instead.

Daniel, of Book the ninth book of the **Ketuvim**, the holy writings, placed between the books of **Esther** and **Ezra**. The first six chapters deal with events in Daniel's own life; chapters 7–12 describe visions he saw.

David (*da-vid* c. 1030–960 BCE) a shepherd boy anointed by **Samuel** to be Israel's second king. David became a national hero by killing Goliath, a gigantic Philistine soldier, in one-to-one combat. He subsequently married King **Saul's** daughter. As David's military reputation grew, Saul became jealous and made several attempts to kill him. After Saul's death at the Battle of Mount Gilboa, David's own tribe, Judah, acknowledged him as king and he reigned in Hebron. Seven years later, the northern tribes also accepted him and he reigned as king for a further 33 years until his death at the age of 70. He made Jerusalem his capital. David spent much of his reign at war, first wiping out the Philistine threat then conquering other hostile neighbours. By the end of his reign, he had established a small empire. David's greatest ambition had been to build a Temple, but God would not permit this since he had waged wars and shed blood. It was to be built by his son, **Solomon** instead. However, David prepared some of the building materials and composed psalms for use in the Temple.

Dayan (*da-yan*) a judge in a rabbinic court, plural dayanim (*da-yan-im*) . ▶ See also **bet din**. In addition to the standard rabbinic training, dayanim are required to have a thorough knowledge of those areas of Jewish law contained in **Even Haezer** and **Choshen Mishpat**.

Dead Sea Scrolls Hebrew scrolls, written by a Jewish sect that flourished between 200 BCE and the mid first century CE, and hidden in caves above the Dead Sea. The first cave was discovered in 1947, and ten more in the following years. Among the scrolls are copies of nearly every book of the Bible. They are the oldest copies known. Other scrolls, describing the beliefs and practices of the sect, tell us how they lived a monk-like existence in their desert settlement and how they prayed and waited for God to send an army of angels to drive the Romans out, after which they expected to return to purify Jerusalem. They probably hid their scrolls as they fled from the Romans but they never returned. ► See also **Essenes**.

Deborah Hebrew Devorah (*de-vo-rah*), **Judge** and prophetess of the late 12th century BCE. Deborah lived at a time when the Israelites were oppressed by a group of Canaanite kings. Their iron chariots terrified the Israelites who, at that time, had only bronze weapons. She called Barak, an experienced commander, to gather an army and meet the Canaanite forces but he only agreed to go if Deborah would go with him. Together, they inflicted a crushing defeat on the Canaanites. Deborah's victory song is today read as one of the **haftarot**, public scriptural readings.

Deuteronomy Greek, *deuteros nomos*, second law; so called because it contains a repetition of laws given in the earlier books of the **Torah**. It is the fifth book of the Bible, called

Devarim in Hebrew, as well as **Mishneh Torah**, the repetition of the Torah. For details see next entry.

Devarim (*de-var-im*) the fifth book of the **Tenakh**, the Jewish Bible; called Deuteronomy in English. Devarim takes the form of speeches made by **Moses** on the borders of the **Promised Land**. It contains many laws as well as ethical teachings and ends with Moses' death. Devarim is also called **Mishneh Torah**, the repetition of the Torah.

Devekut (*de-ve-koot*) lit. attachment, a central idea in the teachings of Rabbi Yisrael **Baal Shem Tov**, who insisted that the purpose of all Jewish observances was to attach oneself to God. At its most intense, devekut is an experience of total oneness with God such as can be achieved through prayer with concentration and devotion. ► See also **kavannah**.

Dialogue a central idea in the philosophy of Martin **Buber**. For him, dialogue differs from conversation – in coversation people may talk without concentrating fully on what is being said. They withhold part of themselves and are not truly in touch with the other person. Dialogue requires openness to receive what the other is giving and to enter into a profound relationship. Buber taught that people can enter into dialogue with God if they are open enough to let Him into their lives.

Diaspora Greek, dispersion, a collective term for all Jewish settlements outside of the **Holy Land**. ▶ See also **galut, golah**.

Dreidle (*drei-dle*) **Yiddish**, a four-sided spinning top with Hebrew letters on each side (called **sevivon** in Hebrew). Dreidle is a traditional children's game played on **Hanukah**.

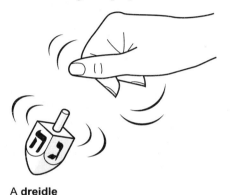

A **dreidle**

It is said to have originated in the second century BCE, when King **Antiochus** IV tried to ban **Torah** study. Classes would study in secret and, whenever soldiers came by, the children would pretend to be playing with their spinning tops.

Dreyfus trial Alfred Dreyfus (1859–1935) was an officer in the French army who, in 1895, was convicted of treason and sent to Devil's Island. Dreyfus' conviction sparked off a wave of anti-Jewish feeling throughout France. It shocked Theodor **Herzl**, then working as a journalist covering the trial, and convinced him that **anti-semitism** would not disappear until Jews had a country of their own. He set down his ideas in his booklet **Der Judenstaat**. Dreyfus was later proved innocent and pardoned.

E

Ecclesiastes, Book of Hebrew Kohelet (*ko-he-let*) , one of the **Chamesh Megilot**, the Five Scrolls. The book examines human life, pausing to discuss people's attempts to attain wealth, love and wisdom. Having considered all these things,

it concludes that all ambition is ultimately futile since humans can neither understand nor change what God has planned. Ecclesiastes ends with the advice, 'Fear God and keep His commandments for this is the whole of man.' According to the

Talmud, Ecclesiastes was written by King **Solomon**. It is read in the synagogue during **Sukkot**.

Echah (*e-chah*) ▶ see **Lamentations**.

Edot (*e-dot*) lit. testimonies: commandments in the Torah which testify to God's care for humankind in general and the Jewish people in particular. Examples of edot are the **Sabbath**, which testifies to God's creation of the world (Genesis 2:3) and **Passover**, which commemorates the Israelites' release from Egyptian slavery. ▶ See also **chukim**, **mishpatim**.

Elijah Hebrew Eliyahu (*e-li-ya-hu*) a miracle-working prophet of the mid 9th century BCE. He fought against the Baal worship introduced by Jezebel, wife of King Ahab. Elijah held a contest on Mount Carmel in front of thousands of Israelites, where the prophets of Baal were invited to select a bull as an offering and pray to their god to send down fire. By late afternoon, when they were weary, Elijah soaked his own offering with water and prayed for fire. A sudden fireball consumed not only the offering but also the water and the stones of the altar. Elijah then commanded the Israelites to kill the 400 prophets of Baal. After this, he fled from Jezebel's anger and went to Mount Horeb (another name for **Mount Sinai**) where he asked God to take his life. There, God gave him his final instructions, which included anointing **Elisha** as his successor. ▶ See also **prophets**.

Elijah, Rabbi of Vilna (1720–1797) called the Vilna Gaon, the genius of Vilna; a child prodigy who became the leader of Lithuanian Jewry and a role model for generations of **yeshivah** students. Rabbi Elijah spent days and nights in seclusion, studying the **Torah**. His study method involved establishing the correct version of the Talmudic text and applying the rules of grammar and the science of his day. He wrote no books, but did jot down personal notes which his students subsequently published. Rabbi Elijah was strongly opposed to the (then) new **Hasidic** movement, refusing to meet their leaders and even pronouncing the ban (excommunication) on them. His followers closed down hasidic synagogues and burnt their books. See also ▶ **mitnagdim**.

Elisha (*e-li-sha*) miracle working prophet of the late 9th century BCE, successor to **Elijah** (II Kings 2:15). Elisha concluded Elijah's work by anointing Jehu as king of Israel. At Elisha's instructions, Jehu brought about the downfall of Jezebel and the House of Ahab.

Elul (*e-lul*) sixth month of the Jewish year, corresponding roughly with August–September. First Elul begins a 40 day period of repentance which ends with **Yom Kippur**, the Day of Atonement. Throughout Elul, the **shofar**, ram's horn, is blown every day (except on Sabbaths and the last day of the month), and **Psalm** 27 is read twice a day. During the latter part of the month, **selichot**, prayers for forgiveness, are said. In some **Sephardi** communities, selichot are said throughout the entire month.

Emancipation granting citizenship, without legal disabilities. Throughout the Middle Ages, the Jews of Europe had no rights and were often subject to humiliating laws and special taxes. During the 18th century, enlightened thinkers pointed out that this was mainly the result of religious prejudice and was unbecoming for men of reason. Some Jews, most notably, **Moses Mendelssohn**, actively campaigned for civic equality. In the latter part of the century, some countries did relax their anti-Jewish laws, but it was the French Revolution – proclaiming liberty, equality and fraternity – that made it possible for Jews to become citizens of a modern state, with full civic rights. During the years that followed, other West European states gradually granted their Jews more and more freedom. ▶ See also **Haskalah, Judenfrage, Sofer**.

En sof lit. without end, a **kabbalistic** term for that aspect of God's Being which is unknowable (as opposed to that which is knowable, eg God's activity in nature).

Enlightened consciousness a central notion in the philosophy of Claude **Montefiore**, the founder of the **Liberal** Jewish movement, based on his belief that God did not give the **Torah** at Mount Sinai, but that while some parts of it are divinely inspired, others are the product of human minds. In Montefiore's view, when people become 'enlightened', ie study the Jewish sources, they will come to realise which parts of the Torah are divine. On the basis of this, they will decide which Jewish practices to observe.

Erusin the first stage of marriage, often translated as 'betrothal', though this is not correct. For details, see **nisuin**.

Eser makot (*e-ser ma-kot*) the ten plagues God inflicted upon the Egyptians to induce them to let the Israelite slaves go free. They were: **1)** all the water in Egypt turned to blood, **2)** swarms of frogs, **3)** swarms of flies, **4)** wild, dangerous animals roaming loose, **5)** a plague that struck the Egyptians' animals, **6)** boils, **7)** hail that destroyed the crops, **8)** swarms of locusts that consumed whatever remained from the hail, **9)** darkness, **10)** killing of all first born Egyptian sons.

Essenes a pietist sect in 1st century Judea. The name derives from an **Aramaic** word meaning healer, since they were skilled in the use of herbs. Most Essenes lived in their own quarters of certain towns. They were very concerned about purity and wore white clothes and frequently immersed themselves in rivers. Some Essenes did not marry. Many scholars think that **Qumran**, near the Dead Sea, was a community of

Essenes and that they were responsible for writing the **Dead Sea Scrolls**.

Esther Persian *Stara*, a star. A young Jewish woman named Hadassah, cousin of Mordecai, a prominent Jewish leader, who became a queen of Ahasuerus, also known as Xerxes I, Emperor of Persia(486–465). She thwarted an attempt by the Grand Vizier to annihilate all the Jews of the Persian Empire. ► See also **Haman**, **Purim**.

Esther, Book of one of the **Chamesh Megillot**, the five scrolls. The book began as a letter, written by Esther and Mordecai (see previous entry) asking the Jews of the Persian Empire to celebrate their deliverance from threat of annihilation (Esther 9: 20–22). They later expanded the letter into a book (see verse 29), giving a full account of the events. ► See also **Haman**, **Purim**.

Ethical monotheism the belief that the one God demands that people live by high ethical standards, through which they can improve the world. The idea was central to the thought of the German-Jewish philosopher, Hermann Cohen (1842–1918), and influenced later Reform thinkers, who took it to mean that God demands ethical behaviour rather than the performance of those commandments that have no obvious connection with moral conduct. ► See also **Baeck**.

Etrog (*et-rog*) citron, one of the **arbaat haminim**, the four plant species used during the prayers on **Sukkot**.

Etz chaim (*etz cha-yim*) lit. tree of life, one of the two wooden poles around which the **Torah scroll** is wound, plural atzei chaim (*a-tzei cha-yim*). The ends of the scroll are stitched to the atzei chaim. The two poles are used for holding the scroll when carrying it as Jews try to avoid handling the parchment itself, as well as for winding it back and forth.

A Torah scroll showing the **atzei chaim** or wooden poles at each end.

Even Haezer (*e-ven Ha-e-zer*) lit. the rock of sustenance, the third part of the two important law **codes, Arbaah Turim** and **Shulchan Aruch**. Even Haezer deals with matrimonial law and includes betrothal, marriage and divorce.

Exilarch lit. head of the exile (a translation of the **Aramaic** title *resh galuta*); Jewish princes who presided over the Jewish communities that remained in **Babylon** after the exile. The exilarchs were administrative rather than religious authorities (the latter being the **geonim**, whom the exilarchs appointed). Their residence at Ctesiphon on the River Tigris, an enormous estate with a palace and servants, gave the Jewish community a high degree of prestige. The exilarchs' most valuable function was to protect Jews in their dealings with the Persian authorities who ruled Babylon.

Exodus the second book of the Bible; so called since it describes the Israelites' departure (*exodus* in Greek) from slavery in Egypt; called **Shemot** in Hebrew.

Ezekiel Hebrew Yechezkiel (*ye-chez-ki-el*) a prophet whose career spanned the years before and after the destruction of the first **Temple**. He was exiled to **Babylon** at the age of 25. Ezekiel is one of the most difficult prophets to understand, in particular his descriptions of heavenly scenes, his symbolic actions (which he sometimes leaves unexplained) and his plan for a rebuilt Temple in the **messianic** future. Ezekiel foretold the destruction of Jerusalem, teaching that it was necessary if a new order was to be built. After the destruction, he acted as counsellor to those whose faith had been shaken by it, having to justify God's justice to those who complained that they had been punished for their fathers' sins. His prophecy of a renewed future for the Jewish people is expressed in a beautiful vision of a valley of dry bones, where God joins them together, puts skin on them and makes them live once more in their own land. ▶ See also **Babylonian exile**.

Ezekiel, Book of the 9th book of the **Neviim**, the prophets. It falls into two broad parts; the first part, chapters 1–24 are prophecies of the destruction of **Jerusalem** and the exile of the people of **Judah**. It subdivides as follows: chapters 1:1–3:21, Ezekiel's call to be a prophet; 3:22– end of chapter 7, the destruction of Judah; chapters 8–19 the reasons for the coming destruction; chapters 20–24 further prophecies of Judah's doom. The second part is concerned mainly with restoration. Chapters 25–32 foretell the destruction of other nations, including Egypt and Judah's old enemies, Ammon, Moab and Edom, assuring the Jews that they will not fear them any longer; chapters 33–39 are prophecies of comfort and restoration; the last eight chapters describe the future, rebuilt **Temple**.

Ezra a scribe, of priestly descent, who worked with **Nehemiah** during the late 5th century BCE to rebuild the Jerusalem community after the return from **Babylonian exile**. Ezra completed the building of the second Temple, started some years earlier by Zerubbabel but stopped by the Persian authorities. Ezra re-established the **Torah** as the community's guide to life, clamping down on **out-marriage** and compelling Jews who had taken heathen wives to send them away. Later Jewish tradition taught that if the Torah had not been given through **Moses** it would have been given through Ezra.

Ezra, Book of written in late classical **Hebrew**, with sections in Aramaic where it quotes from official Persian documents (**Aramaic** was the language of international diplomacy during the period of the Persian Empire; 539–333 BCE) and also some Persian words and phrases. It describes the rebuilding of the Temple, giving an account of trouble with the Samaritans, who tried to get the project stopped and Ezra's negotiations with the Persian authorities.

F

Falashas Amharic for exiles; Ethiopians who claim descent from King **Solomon** and observe many Jewish customs in some form. Their Bible (which they read in the Ge'ez language) comprises the whole of the **Tenakh** as well as some books of the **Apocrypha**. Falashas began emigrating to Israel in 1955. In 1980, when it became known that those in Ethiopia were being persecuted, Israel decided to airlift them out. Due to intermarriage in Ethiopia, there was some doubt about their Jewish status and many of those arriving in Israel were required to undergo a **conversion**.

Family Purity ▶ see **taharat hamishpachah**.

Final Solution the **Nazis'** so-called solution to the **Jewish Question**, ie the question of whether Jews can be loyal citizens of a modern state. Nazi thinkers reasoned that earlier solutions such as **emancipation**, granting Jews civic rights or **assimilation**, trying to absorb them into the rest of the population, had failed. For them, there was only one solution ie to eliminate them entirely so that the world would be **Judenrein**, clean of Jews. In September 1941, the mass extermination began. ▶ See also **Auschwitz**, **Judenfrage** and map 4.

Frank, Anne (1929–1945) a Jewish girl who became famous for her diary, published after her death.

When the **Nazis** came to power in 1933, the Frank family left Germany and moved to Holland. In 1942, the Nazis began deporting the Dutch Jews to concentration camps in Poland and Anne, together with her parents, younger sister and four other Jews, were hidden by non-Jewish friends. Just over two years later, they were discovered and sent to Bergen-Belsen concentration camp. There, in March 1945, Anne caught typhus and died. She was 16 years old. Her diary, describing the experiences of the eight Jews during their two years of hiding, was published after the war and translated into many languages. Since then, Anne Frank has become a symbol, for Jews and non-Jews alike, of childhood destroyed by tyranny. ▶ See also **Shoah**.

Frankel, Zacharias (1801–1875)

founder of the 'positive–historical' school of thought which maintained that Judaism had always changed with time and that changes were beneficial. Frankel never really reconciled his traditional Talmudic education with his philosophical studies in university. He was attacked by the extreme reformers because he objected to the radical changes they were introducing into Judaism. He also aroused the anger of the **Orthodox**, in particular of Rabbi Samson Raphael **Hirsch** who challenged him to give a clear statement of his views on the origin of the Torah. Frankel preferred to sidestep these questions rather than answer them. His views later became very influential in the **Conservative** movement in America which (originally) called for slight reforms, as well as in the British **Masorti Movement**.

G

Gabbai (*ga-bai*) lit. treasurer, originally the person who ran the community's finances and was responsible for distributing food and money to the poor. Today, the gabbai co-ordinates the services in the synagogue.

Galut (*ga-lut*) lit. exile, the **diaspora**; also called the **golah**. Jews tend to use galut to mean spiritual exile, ie the condition of being spiritually deprived; golah usually refers to the physical exile, ie the fact of being in other countries. Hence,

Jews in Israel are not living in the golah, though they may still be in a condition of galut.

Gaon (*ga-on*) lit. excellency. **1)** title given to the heads of the Babylonian academies between the 5th and 11th centuries; plural geonim (*ge-o-**nim***) **2)** a term of esteem used for an exceptional Talmudic scholar; roughly equivalent of genius. The term 'The Gaon' always refers to the Vilna Gaon, Rabbi **Elijah of Vilna** (1720–1797).

Gehenom Hell; Hebrew *ge hinom*, the valley of Hinom, a valley outside **Jerusalem** where executions took place in the period of the first Temple (10th–6th centuries BCE). By the second Temple period (late 6th century BCE) the term had replaced Sheol as the common name for Hell. In Jewish thought, Gehenom is not a place of everlasting torments but rather a process of cleansing souls from sin and preparing them for entry into the presence of God.

Geiger, Abraham (1810–1874) one of the most influential of the early **Reform** thinkers. Geiger was bitterly opposed to **Orthodoxy**, which he regarded as incapable of inspiring cultured German Jews. Originally, he dreamt of dismantling the whole of Jewish ritual and remodelling the synagogue service on that of the Lutheran Church. In the congregation he served, he discontinued prayers for a return to Zion and even considered abolishing **circumcision**. However, he agreed to retain **Hebrew** as the main language of prayer while introducing some prayers in German. His main contributions to the development of **Reform** were his part in organising conferences where the ideals of the new movement were worked out and his development of a theory of evolution of Judaism.

Gemara (*ge-ma-ra*) **Aramaic**, learning, a name for the Talmudic discussions that form a commentary and expansion on the **Mishnah**; often used to mean the **Talmud** as a whole.

Gematria Greek for calculation; ie using the letters of the Hebrew alphabet as numbers. The first nine letters are used as symbols for numbers 1–9, the next nine letters represent 20, 30, 40... until 90, and the last four letters stand for 100, 200, 300 and 400. Higher numbers are represented by putting letters together; for example, the number 817 would be expressed as 400+400+10+7. Combinations of letters that make up God's name are avoided, other combinations being substituted.

Gemilut hassadim (*ge-mil-**ut** ha-sa-**dim***) lit. giving kindness, a general term for good deeds, helping the sick and disabled, visiting the elderly and housebound, as opposed to **tzedakah**, helping people with donations of money. Good deeds are only called gemilut hassadim when they are done voluntarily.

Genesis the first book of the Bible; so called since it opens with the story of how God created the world – Genesis is Greek for 'beginning', called **Bereshit** in Hebrew.

Genevat daat (*ge-ne-vat da-at*) lit. stealing the mind, ie deception, leading a person to believe that something is true without actually making a false statement. For example, a shop giving customers plastic bags with the words 'London, Paris, New York, Rome, Tokyo' printed at the bottom. The bag does not actually state that there are branches in those cities, but the names create the impression that the shop is part of a major international chain. Genevat daat is forbidden in Jewish law.

Genizah (*ge-ni-zah*) part of a Jewish cemetery where Torah scrolls and holy books are buried once they become too worn or too damaged for further use. Some older synagogues use an attic room as a genizah.

Ger lit. one who dwells (with us), a convert to Judaism, feminine geyoret (*ge-yor-et*).

Gerut (*ge-rut*) the process of becoming Jewish. A non-Jew wanting to convert needs time to learn about Judaism and to adjust to living as a Jew. The conversion is carried out under the supervision of a **bet din**, a rabbinic court. Gerut requires circumcision for a male, immersion in a **mikveh** and formal acceptance of the 613 **mitzvot**, commandments, for males and females. When the **Temple** stood, a convert was also required to offer a sacrifice as part of the conversion procedure. A person undergoing gerut remains Jewish for life since a conversion cannot normally be annulled.

Get a document of divorce. Unlike English law, where a divorce is granted by a court, a Jewish divorce takes place through the actions of the husband and wife themselves. This is because, in **halakhah**, Jewish law, no-one may be compelled to divorce or be divorced. The divorce takes effect from the moment the wife or her representative receives the get from the husband or his representative. The get, which is written especially for the occasion by a scribe, must be freely given and freely received. A civil divorce has no validity in Jewish law. ▶ See also **sofer**.

Ghetto section of a town where Jews were compelled to live, often separated from the rest of the town by a wall. The first ghetto is thought to have been established in Venice in the 16th century, from where the idea spread to the rest of Europe. The last ghettos were wiped out during the Holocaust. In recent years, the term has come to be used, usually in a derogatory sense, to refer to areas where large numbers of Jews live.

Gideon Hebrew Gidon (*gi-don*) a **Judge** of the 11th century BCE. God called Gideon to beat off attacks from Midianite tribes. Gideon found it hard to believe that God had actually chosen him and asked for a sign. He left a sheep's fleece on the ground at night asking for it to be wet with dew while the ground was dry; the following night he asked for the opposite to happen. After both signs had been given, Gideon struck the enemy camp with a small force of picked men and drove them away. Later, the Israelites wanted to make Gideon king but he refused.

Golah (*go-lah*) exile; ▶ see **galut**.

H

Habad (*ha-bad*) (also spelt Chabad) a word formed from the initial letters of hochmah (wisdom), binah (understanding) and daat (knowledge), used to refer to the philosophy of Rabbi Shneur Zalman of Liadi (1745–1813). Habad is a branch of the **Hasidic Movement**. Its basic teaching is that it is possible for the human mind to understand more about God and His relationship with the world than is often realised and that it is not sufficient to rely on faith alone in matters that can be grasped by the intellect. Followers of Habad do not see this as a purely intellectual pursuit but rather as a way of enhancing the way they serve God and achieving holiness in everyday life. ▶ See also **Schneerson**.

Habakkuk Hebrew (*ha-va-kook*) a prophet of the early 6th century BCE.

Habakkuk addressed the crisis of faith that arose as a result of the Babylonian invasion of **Judah** – ie how could God be in control of events if the Babylonians have conquered His city? Habakkuk's message was that the Babylonians were actually the instruments of God's anger and that He had used them to punish the sinful people of Judah. He taught that God is always in control and would eventually judge the Babylonians for their excesses.

Habakkuk, Book of the 8th book in **Trei Asar**, the Twelve Prophets. Much of the book takes the form of a dialogue between Habakkuk and God. The prophet questions God's justice, asking how He can let the wicked Babylonians prosper while the comparatively innocent people of Judah are being oppressed. God explains that He has events under control and that people will learn important moral lessons from the Babylonians' excesses. The last chapter depicts God preparing for the final judgement in which His people will be saved.

Hadas (*ha-das*) myrtle branch, plural hadassim (*ha-da-sim*). Three hadassim are bound with one palm branch and two sprigs of willow as part of the **arbaat haminim**, the four plant species Jews use during the prayers of **Sukkot**.

Haftarah (*haf-ta-rah*) lit. parting, a passage from one of the books of the **Neviim** (Prophets) read after the **Torah** reading on Sabbaths, festivals and fast days; plural haftarot (*haf-ta-rot*). The passages chosen have some connection with the contents of the Torah reading, the persons mentioned therein or to the occasion on which they are read. While there is some variation in custom between **Ashkenazi** (western) and **Sephardi** (eastern) communities, most passages selected for haftarot are universal.

Haggadah (*ha-ga-dah*) lit. telling, a collection of teachings relating to the Israelite's slavery in Egypt and their miraculous departure; plural haggadot (*ha-ga-dot*). The hagadah is read at the **seder**, the Passover meal, as a means of generating a discussion – as the haggadah itself puts it, 'all who discuss the departure from Egypt at length are praiseworthy'.

Haggai a prophet of the 5th century BCE, who urged those who had returned from **Babylonian exile** to rebuild the **Temple**; a contemporary of **Zechariah**. His recorded prophecies date from 1st Ellul to 24th Kislev in 520 BCE, ie a period of just under four months. Addressing the poverty of the new Jerusalem community, he tells them that their sufferings are due to the fact they have neglected their holy work. He assures them that the Temple they were to build would be greater than the first one, and refers to the words of hope in the prophecies of **Isaiah**, **Jeremiah** and **Ezekiel**.

Haggai, Book of the 10th book of **Trei Asar**, the Twelve Prophets. It is a short book, containing only 38 verses, but full of encouragement for the Jews who had recently returned from exile and who were working to rebuild Jerusalem.

Hakafah (*ha-ka-fah*) lit. circuit, plural hakafot (*ha-ka-fot*) **1)** each day of **Sukkot**, after the **Hallel** prayer, worshippers circle the synagogue in a procession holding their **arbaat haminim**, four plant species. On **Hoshanah Rabbah** they make seven circuits. **2)** On **Shemini Atzeret** and **Simchat Torah**, worshippers circle the synagogue in a joyous procession holding **Torah scrolls**. **3)** In some communities, a bride circles her husband seven times at the beginning of the wedding ceremony.

Hakotel Hamaaravi (*ha-ko-tel ha-ma-a-ra-vi*) lit. the western wall;

the last wall still remaining from the Roman destruction of Jerusalem and the 2nd Temple in 70 CE. It is also known as the Wailing Wall since Jews used to go there to mourn for the loss of **Jerusalem** and the Temple. For many years, the wall was in Jordanian hands and Jews were not permitted to visit it. In 1967, Jews regained possession of it. It is Judaism's most sacred site, with thousands of worshippers praying there every day.

Halakhah (*ha-la-khah*) lit. a going, guidelines for living as a Jew, often referred to as 'Jewish law', plural halakhot (*ha-la-chot*). It is used both as a collective term referring to the whole of Jewish law as well as to individual laws. Halakhah is one of the most important instruments for Jewish living, since Jews believe that God is to be served through the ordinary acts of everyday life and that everything can be done in a way that is either consistent or inconsistent with God's will.

Halakhic relating to or concerning the **halakhah** (see previous entry).

Hallel (*ha-lel*) a recitation of Psalms 113–118, take place on certain festivals . On **Rosh Chodesh**, the beginning of a new month, and also the last days of Passover, only part Hallel is said. On **Sukkot**, Jews hold their **arbaat haminim**, four plant species, during Hallel.

Haman a Grand Vizier of Ahasuerus (486-465 BCE), Emperor of Persia. Haman had been a leading figure in the Troublers of Judah and Benjamin (Ezra 4:1), an anti-Jewish action group that had tried to prevent Jews resettling in the **Holy Land** after the destruction of the first **Temple**. As Grand Vizier, he used the excuse of a prominent Jew not bowing to him to order the massacre of all the Jews in the Empire. The attempt was thwarted by **Esther**, a Jewish queen of Ahasuerus, and Haman was executed. ▶ See also **Purim**.

Hametz (*ha-metz*) grain products that have swollen or are capable of swelling by the action of yeasts. Jews are neither permitted to eat nor to own hametz during Passover. The swelling hametz is a symbol of pride, whereas the lesson of Passover is humility in recognition that the Israelites were totally dependent on God for their release from Egyptian slavery. ▶ See also **bedikat hametz**, **Pesach**.

Hanukah (*ha-noo-kah*) lit. dedication, also spelt Chanukah; an eight-day celebration that commemorates the Jews' victory over **Antiochus** IV, ruler of the Seleucid Empire, who tried to abolish Judaism. Hanukah marks the rededication of the **Temple** after it had been taken over for heathen worship. It is celebrated by lighting oil lamps or candles – one light on the first night, two the second and so on up to eight. It recalls the miracle that took place after the Jews recaptured the Temple and lit the oil lamp with a small amount of oil that should only have burnt for one night and burned for eight instead. ▶ See also **Maccabean revolt, Menorah**.

Hanukiah (*ha-noo-kee-ah*) lamp used during **Hanukah**; also called **menorah**. A hanukiah is made to contain eight candles or oil-burning wicks, with an additional container for the **shamash**, the servant candle, used to light the others.

Haroset (*ha-ro-set*) a paste made from crushed apples or pears, almonds, cinnamon and wine, used at the **seder**, the Passover meal. Some **Sephardim**, oriental Jews, make it by boiling dates to a thick syrup. It has the appearance of river mud, which the Israelite slaves used to make bricks. In classical Jewish literature, the ingredients are used as metaphors referring to the Jewish people.

Hashem lit. the name, a word Jews use when referring to God in everyday conversation, since they regard God's names as holy and only pronounce them in prayer. In effect, Hashem means 'the one whose name is not mentioned unnecessarily'.

Hasid (*ha-sid*) member of a Hasidic community, plural Hasidim (*ha-si-dim*). Most Hasidim are easily recognisable by their dress – the men in 19th century, East European style black coats, black hats and (sometimes) knee-length breeches, the women dressed very modestly in

wrist-length sleeves and thick stockings. The men also have long side curls. Their spoken language is **Yiddish**, though men tend to use it more than women. They generally live quiet, pious lives, are hard working and like to keep themselves to themselves. One group of Hasidim, the followers of **Habad**, wear 20th century clothes and often have a good secular education (some are university professors). Unlike other Hasidim, they seek contact with people and regard it as their duty to make other Jews aware of God's commandments.

Hasidic Movement (*cha-sid-dic*) a revivalist movement founded by Rabbi Israel **Baal Shem Tov** (1698–1760) in Poland. Rabbi Israel's teachings brought renewed hope to Jews broken by years of hardship and, within his own lifetime, his followers numbered thousands. During the years following his death, the movement spread right across Eastern Europe. During the **Holocaust**, the Hasidim suffered appalling losses. Many fled and re-established their communities in other countries. Today, the Hasidic movement comprises many groups – some of them numbering hundreds of thousands and settled in various parts of the world, others quite small and restricted to a particular locality. The different groups call themselves by the names of the East European towns from where they originated and are distinguished from one another by slight variations in custom.

Hasidut (*ha-si-dut*) the teachings of the Hasidic movement. Hasidut began with Rabbi Yisrael **Baal Shem Tov** (1698–1760) and continued through the sayings and writings of the hasidic masters (▶ see **Rebbe**) to the present day. Although different forms of hasidut developed in different branches of the movement, certain themes are common to them all, eg the intimate relationship between God and His creation, the unique role of the Jewish people and the cosmic significance of performing the **mitzvot**, commandments.

Haskalah (*has-ka-lah*) the movement, that began in the late 18th century, aimed at integrating Jews into general society; also known as the 'Jewish enlightenment'. Throughout the Middle Ages, most Jews in Europe lived as a people apart, with their own form of dress and their own language (**Yiddish**). Their education consisted solely of religious subjects. Jews who did mix in non-Jewish circles, particularly in Germany, sometimes felt inadequate since they could not converse with cultured non-Jews on equal terms. A trend to acquire non-Jewish culture took shape around **Moses Mendelssohn** and became known as haskalah. Those who followed his lead (called **maskilim**) encouraged Jews to dress like everyone else, learn modern languages and accept the need to study **secular** subjects. They also wrote scientific books in Hebrew to introduce other Jews to modern knowledge. Many maskilim regarded these changes necessary if Jews were to achieve emancipation through civic rights. Most religious authorities opposed haskalah, fearing that it would lead to **assimilation** (which, to a large degree, it did). Some followers of haskalah called for changes in Judaism, giving rise to the **Reform** movement. A fusion of traditional **Orthodoxy** and haskalah emerged as **Neo-Orthodoxy**. ▶ See also **Samson Raphael Hirsch**.

Hatikvah (*ha-tik-vah*) lit. The Hope, national anthem of Israel. Hatikvah began as as poem written by Naftali Hertz Imber in 1878 called Tikvatenu, Our Hope. In 1882 it was set to a Moldavian–Rumanian folk tune (the same folk tune Smetena used in his 'Voltava'). In this form it was adopted at the 18th Zionist Congress in 1933 as the anthem of the Zionist Movement and, after 1948, became the national anthem of the Jewish State.

Havdalah (*hav-da-lah*) lit. separation, a ceremony to mark the conclusion of Sabbath or a festival. It requires a cup of wine (certain other drinks are also suitable), spices and a candle, plaited so that several wicks mingle to produce the flame. First, a blessing is said over the wine (compare **kiddush** at the commencement of the Sabbath or festive meal), followed by a blessing over spices (which everyone smells) symbolising that something spiritual has departed, and a blessing over the flame, signifying that Jews may light fire once more (lighting fire is forbidden on the Sabbath, ▶ see **melachah**). Finally, there is a blessing thanking God for providing a holy day of rest and separating it from the weekdays. When havdalah is performed at the conclusion of a festival, the blessings over the spices and flame are omitted.

The plaited candle, wine and spices used during **havdalah**.

Hebrew the principal language of the **Tenakh**, the Jewish Bible and the traditional Jewish language of prayer, also known as **leshon hakodesh**, the holy tongue; closely related to **Aramaic**. Hebrew has passed through four main stages: **1)** Classical Hebrew, the Hebrew of the Bible and contemporary inscriptions lasted till about the 5th century BCE. This was the golden age of Hebrew poetry which had a lofty, majestic style. During the latter part of this period, Aramaic began to be more commonly used (▶ see **Daniel,**

Ezra); **2)** Mishnaic Hebrew, the language of the **Mishnah** (2nd century CE) had adopted many Aramaic forms of expression and was more terse than the classical language; **3)** Medieval Hebrew, no longer a spoken language but used mainly for Torah study. The religious poets of this period produced the **selichot**, prayers for forgiveness and the **kinot**, dirges; **4)** Modern Hebrew, the spoken language of the State of Israel (▶ see Ivrit). The roots of the modern language lie in the writings of the **maskilim**, the 18th and 19th century **secularists**, in particular Eliezer **ben Yehudah**.

Hechal (*he-chal*) lit. palace or temple, name used for the ark in some **Sephardi** (oriental) synagogues.

Hechsher (*hech-sher*) a stamp or seal certifying that a food product is **kosher**. In the past, it was relatively easy to know which foods were kosher and which not. Today, the use of food additives has complicated matters since these substances are extracted from a variety of sources, not all of them kosher. To overcome this, rabbis (often with training in food science) supervise the manufacture of certain foods and ensure that all the ingredients are kosher or derived from kosher sources. The food packet, can or carton will bear a hechsher, a stamp affirming that it is so. For a hechsher to be valid, it must state the name of the rabbi or rabbinical board responsible for the supervision.

LONDON BETH-DIN

A **hechsher**.

Herzl, Theodor (1860–1904) a Viennese journalist who founded the World Zionist Organisation. Herzl had a very assimilated upbringing and at one time believed that the solution to the 'Jewish Question' (▶ see **Judenfrage**) was for all Jews to accept Roman Catholicism. Herzl's life changed through the wave of **anti-semitism** unleashed in the wake of the **Dreyfus** trial in 1885, which convinced him that anti-semitism would only stop when Jews had a land of their own. He set his ideas down in Der **Judenstaat**, published the following year. Herzl spent his remaining years travelling widely, trying to gain the political support of influential figures (including the German Kaiser and the Grand Vizier of the Ottoman Empire) and the financial support of Jewish philanthropists such as Barons Hirsch and Rothschild. He was rebuffed time and again, even by some of the **Hovovei Zion** – the very people who were working to

resettle Jews in **Palestine**. In spite of all opposition, he convened an international conference in Basle in 1897 which adopted the resolution to create a Jewish homeland in Palestine. Herzl was elected head of the newly formed World Zionist Organisation, a position he held until his death at the age of 44. ▶ See also **Hibat Zion**, **Zionism**.

Hesped (*hes-ped*) eulogy, a speech at a funeral, in which rabbis or other religious leaders extol the piety, scholarship, self-sacrifice or other virtues of the deceased, plural hespedim (*hes-pe-dim*). Jews regard hespedim as important since the life of a departed person can be held up as a model for others to emulate. Some people do not want hespedim said at their funerals and, where such wishes are left, they must be honoured.

Hibat Zion (*hi-bat Zi-on*) lit. love of Zion, a movement that emerged in Russia and Rumania in the mid 19th century, and somewhat later in western Europe. Its aim was to settle Jews in **Palestine** as a means of escaping **anti-semitism**. Its supporters were known as **Hovovei Zion**, lovers of Zion. The Hovovei Zion had no plan for setting up an independent Jewish state, though individual leaders did believe that the Jewish settlers should have some form of self government (▶ see **Lillienblum**). After the **pogroms** of the 1880s, their task became particularly urgent. However, they never had sufficient finance to support large scale resettlement – that had to wait for Theodor **Herzl** and the rise of **Zionism**. ▶ See also **Ahad Ha'am, Autoemancipation, Mohilever, Pinsker**.

Hildesheimer, Rabbi Azriel
(1820–1899) German rabbi and leader of **Neo-Orthodoxy**. Hildesheimer believed that Jews should study secular subjects as well as **Talmud**. He opened a **yeshivah**, Talmudic academy, on this basis in Eisenstadt, near the Austrio–Hungarian border but the Hungarian rabbis objected to it and it closed down. He moved to Berlin in 1869 and, four years later, established a seminary for training rabbis. Although Hildesheimer was opposed to **Reform**, he believed in co-operation on communal issues such as combating **anti-semitism**. He supported Hibat Zion and raised funds for their projects in **Palestine**.

Hillel (late 1st century BCE and early 1st century CE) known as Hillel the Elder. He was born in **Babylon** and studied in Jerusalem under Shemaya and Avtalyon, the foremost rabbinic leaders of the day. Hillel began the process of classifying the halakhah, Jewish law, that led to the **Mishnah** two centuries later. He formulated seven principles for deriving halachot from scripture. Hillel was famed for his humility and patience, of which there are many stories – for example, the heathen who asked Hillel to teach him the whole Torah standing on one leg. Hillel told him

'Whatever is hateful to you do not do to others. That is the whole of the Torah, the rest is commentary.' He used teaching methods that were unusual for his time, often throwing out challenging questions to trigger off a discussion.

Hirsch, Rabbi Samson Raphael
(1808–1888) German rabbi, the most influential thinker of **Neo-Orthodoxy**. Rabbi Hirsch's slogan was, 'Torah im derekh eretz', a phrase from **Pirke Avot**, lit. Torah study with a worldly occupation, but which he took to mean Torah and **secular** study. His ideal was the **Jissroel-mensch**, the observant, cultured Jew, an ideal he promoted in the three schools he founded. He was the first Orthodox leader to cater for the Jewish education of girls. Rabbi Hirsch was a firm opponent of **Reform**, which he saw as a distortion of Judaism. Nonetheless, he wanted to avoid a formal separation into Orthodox and Reform communities. It was only after the Reform conferences of 1845, when the reformers voted for radical changes in Judaism, that he saw separation as inevitable. ▶ See also **Hildesheimer**.

Holocaust ▶ see **Shoah** and map 4.

Holy of Holies the innermost room of the **mishkan**, the portable temple the Israelites built in the desert and, later, in the **Temple**. In it was the holy ark, a wooden and golden box which contained, among

other things, the blocks of stone bearing the **Ten Commandments** that Moses brought down from **Mount Sinai**. The Holy of Holies was separated from the rest of the Temple by a curtain. Only the High Priest was allowed to enter, and only on **Yom Kippur**, the Day of Atonement, to pray for forgiveness for the people.

Hosea Hebrew (*ho-she-a*) a prophet of the mid 8th century BCE who delivered his message during the closing years of the Kingdom of **Israel**, before its overthrow by Assyria. He railed against the idolatry of the age, using the image of an unfaithful wife. For him, Israel's **covenant** with God was a marriage and, by turning to other gods, Israel was committing adultery. He taught that the Assyrian invasion would come, and that there was no immediate hope for Israel . However, at some future time, God would forgive Israel and restore the covenant.

Hosea, Book of the 1st book of **Trei Asar**, the Twelve Prophets. The early chapters describe the prophet's personal trial – God commanded him to marry a prostitute since he was required to be a living lesson to the people of Israel with an unfaithful wife as a parallel to the nation's idolatry (see previous entry). Chapters 5–14 foretell the punishment of the people of Israel, ending with a call to righteousness.

Hoshanah Rabbah the last day of **Sukkot**; ▶ see next entry.

Hoshanot (*ho-sha-not*) lit. deliverances, including prayers for rain said during **Sukkot**, which occurs at the beginning of the rainy season in the Holy Land. During Hoshanot, worshippers hold their **arbaat haminim**, four plant species, and circle the **bimah**, the platform, just as people would circle the altar in the Temple, ▶ see hakafot. Upon the bimah, someone will be holding a **Torah scroll**. This takes place every day of Sukkot. On the last day, known as **Hoshanah Rabbah**, worshippers make seven circuits.

Hovovei Zion (*ho-vo-vei Zi-on*) lit. lovers of Zion, members of the **Hibat Zion** movement.

Huldah (*hul-dah*) a prophetess of the late 6th century BCE, a contemporary of **Jeremiah**. When King Josiah's workmen discovered a scroll while repairing the Temple, the king consulted Huldah about the prophecies of destruction it contained. She told him that destruction would indeed come, but that it would not happen in his lifetime (see II Kings 22:14–20).

Huppah (*hoo-pah*) the wedding canopy, a covering held up by four posts, under which Jewish weddings take place; also spelt chupah. The huppah symbolises togetherness, since it encloses the couple who stand beneath it, while open on all

sides to remind them that they are
still part of the wider community.
After the huppah, bride and groom
go to a room where they will spend
a short time alone in each other's
company. This, called **yichud**, is a
demonstration that they are husband
and wife, and completes the
ceremony.

Hurban (*hur-ban*) lit. destruction;
1) a term used for the destruction
of the Temple, **2)** another name for
the **Holocaust**. ▶ See **Shoah** and
map 4.

The **huppah** or wedding canopy.

I

Imahot (*i-ma-hot*) lit. mothers,
▶ see **Matriarchs**.

Isaac Hebrew Yitzchak (*yitz-chak*)
son of Abraham and second of the
Patriarchs, the fathers of the Jewish
people. Unlike the other Patriarchs,
Abraham and **Jacob**, Isaac never left
the Holy Land. He married his
cousin, **Rebekah**; they had two sons,
Jacob and Esau. According to
tradition, Isaac was in the habit of
praying in the afternoon and so
instituted the **minchah** prayer.

Isaiah Hebrew Yeshayahu (*ye-sha-ya-hu*) prophet of the late 7th century
BCE. Isaiah began prophesying in
Jerusalem at about the time the
Assyrians threatened to invade, in
742 BCE. Although he involved
himself in the politics of the day by
urging successive kings of Judah to
have faith in God rather than in
political alliances, Isaiah mainly
directed his teaching against the
materialism, corruption and foreign
religious cults he saw all around him.
He cried out against those who

carried out religious rituals without practising justice and righteousness, and warned the people of Jerusalem that if they changed their ways they would prosper; if not they would be destroyed by the sword. Long before the destruction, he spoke of the remnant who would return, purified by the trials they would have gone through.

Isaiah, Book of the first 39 chapters are a record of Isaiah's prophecies, chapters 36–39 retelling the history of Judah and parallelling II Kings 18–19. Chapters 40–66 are prophecies of comfort that look forward to a better future. The messianic age features strongly in these chapters. Some modern scholars have developed a theory that these chapters were not written by Isaiah since they refer to events that happened after his time. They claim that these chapters are the work of an unknown prophet whom they call Deutero-Isaiah, the second Isaiah. Those who reject the theory point out that it is not unreasonable for a prophet to have known of later events.

Israel Hebrew (*yis-ra-el*) **1)** name given to **Jacob** because he 'wrestled with God and man' (Genesis 32: 29); **2)** name of descendants of Jacob, called Benei Yisrael, the Children of Israel (ie Israelites), Jews still refer to the Jewish people as a whole as Israel; **3)** Land of Israel, ie the **Promised Land**, roughly equivalent to the modern State of Israel, but also including territory east of the Jordan, ▶ see map 2; **4)** name of the northern Jewish kingdom after the division that took place following **Solomon's** death; **5)** the modern State of Israel, established in 1948.

Ivrit (*iv-rit*) the Hebrew spoken in modern Israel. ▶ See **Ben Yehudah**.

Iyar (*i-yar*) 2nd month of the Jewish year, corresponding roughly with April–May. There are no festivals in Iyar, but there are several special days – 5th, **Yom Ha'atzmaut**, Israel Independence Day; 14th **Pesach Sheni**, the second Passover; 18th **Lag b'Omer**; 28th **Yom Yerushalayim**, Jerusalem Day.

Jabotinsky, Vladimir (1880–1940) militant Zionist leader who, together with Joseph **Trumpeldor**, organised the Jewish Legion at the end of World War I to liberate **Palestine** from Turkish rule. In 1920, he created the Haganah, the Jewish defence unit, and led it against the Arab rioters during that year's disturbances. He was arrested by the British and sentenced to 15 years hard labour but, due to international pressure, was released the following year. In 1925 he founded the World Union of Zionist Revisionists, whose aim was a return to **Herzl**'s Zionism, which he interpreted as large scale immigration to Palestine and the formation of a Jewish army to safeguard the settlers on both sides of the Jordan. During World War II, he organised underground resistance to British rule in Palestine and assisted 'illegal' immigration.

Jacob Hebrew (*ya-a-kov*) son of Isaac and 3rd of the **Patriarchs**, the fathers of the Jewish people. Jacob took the blessing his father intended to bestow on his older brother, Esau, and then had to run away because his brother wanted to kill him. He worked for his uncle, Laban, for 21 years, during which time he married Laban's two daughters, **Leah** and **Rachel** as well as their

maidservants, Bilhah and Zilpah. Between them they had 12 sons (who established the **twelve tribes** of Israel) and a daughter. At the end of his life, Jacob settled in Egypt. When he died, his sons brought him back to the **Holy Land** to bury him in **Mearat Hamachpelah**, the family tomb in Hebron. According to tradition, Jacob was in the habit of praying last thing at night to thank God for having seen him through the day, and so instituted the idea of **arvit**, the evening prayer.

Jacobs, Louis (b. 1920) the spiritual head of the **Masorti Movement**, formerly rabbi of an **Orthodox** synagogue. In 1957 he published a book in which he outlined his beliefs – that the Torah was not fully revealed to **Moses** at **Mount Sinai** but was partly the work of people recording their encounter with the divine. This caused a major controversy in Anglo–Jewry, resulting in Dr. Jacobs not being appointed to the principalship of Jews' College (a training college for rabbis) and being denied the post of rabbi in an Orthodox synagogue. He subsequently became the spiritual leader of an independent congregation, resulting in the formation of the Masorti Movement.

Jepthah Hebrew Yiftach (*yif-tach*), a judge who led Israel to victory over the Ammonites (Judges 11: 1-12) in the late 11th century BCE. Driven from his home by his half brothers, Jepthah led a wild existence, attracting to himself all sorts of outcasts whom he led, gaining a reputation as a courageous soldier. When the Ammonites threatened to invade, the Israelite elders asked Jepthah to lead them. He agreed on condition that they make him their chief. He tried negotiating with the Ammonites, pointing out that they had no real claim to the territory they sought since God had given it to the Israelites. They pressed their offensive and Jepthah inflicted a crushing defeat on them. Before the battle he had vowed that he would sacrifice to God whatever came out of his house as he returned. To his horror, his only daughter came out to greet him. It is not certain whether he actually sacrificed her.

Jeremiah Hebrew Yirmeyahu (*yir-me-ya-hu*) the outstanding prophet of the late 6th and early 5th centuries BCE. Jeremiah was the most tragic of all the prophets; others had foretold the destruction of Jerusalem and the Temple, he lived to see his prophecies fulfilled. He denounced injustice and the corruption of the leaders, using images of an unfaithful wife to highlight Israel's unfaithfulness to God (compare **Hosea**), and cried out against those who carried out religious rituals without practising righteousness

(compare **Isaiah**), thinking that their rituals alone would stand them in good stead with God. He taught that unless the people of Jerusalem changed their ways, they would be destroyed and the Temple would be lost. Those in power made several attempts to silence him. They forbade him to preach in the Temple, imprisoned him on more than one occasion and even attempted to kill him. Jeremiah would have preferred not to have to deliver prophecies of doom; in one chapter he describes how he tried to hold them back but the prophetic words burned inside him and he was forced to let them out (Jeremiah 20: 9). When the first wave of Jews was deported to Babylon, Jeremiah wrote a letter urging them to build homes, settle down and give up all hope of a quick return. After the assassination of Gedaliah, ▶ see **Tzom Gedaliah**, the fleeing Jews took Jeremiah to Egypt where he died.

Jeremiah, Book of the book contains mainly prophecies of Jeremiah written down by his secretary, Baruch ben Neriah. Chapters 26–29 and 32–44 give a good deal of information about Jeremiah himself.

Jerusalem Hebrew Yerushalayim (*ye-ru-sha-la-yim*) the Jews' holy city. In the time of **Abraham**, the site was a small hilltop settlement called Shalem. Later, when it was occupied by the Jebusites, **David** took it and made it his capital. A generation later, **Solomon**, his son, built the first

Temple there and it has remained the focal point of Jewish spirituality ever since. The Jews' attachment to Jerusalem has never diminished, even when it was captured by foreign powers (the Romans pulled down nearly every building, renamed it Aelia Capitolina and would not allow Jews to enter it) and it has featured in their prayers ever since the **Babylonian exile** in the 6th century BCE. In 1948, it became the capital of the modern State of **Israel**, even though Jews only controlled the western half of the city. On 28th **Iyar** 1967, Jews regained control of the whole of Jerusalem. Many Jews celebrate an annual **Yom Yerushalayim** (Jerusalem Day) on that date.

Jew Hebrew Yehudi (*ye-hu-di*) originally a member of the tribe of **Judah**, later used of inhabitants of the country of Judah. After the Kingdom of **Israel** was exiled by the Assyrians in 722 BCE, the term Yehudi gradually assumed its present day meaning, (compare Esther 3: 4-6).

Jissroel-mensch (*yis-ro-el mench*) German, lit. Israel-man, a term coined by Rabbi Samson Raphael **Hirsch** (1808–1888) to describe his image of the ideal Jew – a person fully committed to Judaism and observing all its commandments faithfully while, at the same time, possessing a broad education and appreciation for general culture.

Job, Book of Hebrew Iyov (*i-yov*) the third book of the **Ketuvim**, the

Holy Writings, it deals with the problem of suffering. It focuses on Job, a pious and wealthy man whom God tests. The first chapter sets the scene; he loses all his wealth, his children die and finally he himself is afflicted with appalling pain. The rest of the book is a series of discussions between Job and his three friends. They insist that his afflictions are all punishment for his sins. Job knows that this is not so but has a hard time convincing them and an even harder time coming to terms with what he can only see as God's injustice. Finally, God appears in a whirlwind. However, instead of answering Job's questions, God simply points out that His ways are beyond human understanding. One purpose of the book is to negate the idea that suffering is necessarily the result of sin. In the **Talmud** and **Midrash**, some rabbis held Job to be a man of exceptional piety; another view is that he did not exist at all and that the book is a parable.

Joel Hebrew Yoel (*yo-el*) it is uncertain when Joel lived. He refers to a devastating plague of locusts that left the people of Judah almost without food. He also prophesied about the 'end of days', when God will bring all the nations together and pass judgement on those who oppressed the Israelites. After this, God will destroy those nations and bring His people back to live in peace and abundance.

Joel, Book of the second book of **Trei Asar**, the Twelve Prophets. The first two chapters deal with a plague of locusts, chapters 3 and 4 talk about the future messianic time.

Jonah Hebrew Yonah (*yo-nah*) a prophet of the mid 8th century BCE; according to tradition, a disciple of **Elisha**, sent by him to anoint Jehu king of **Israel**. Jonah is best known for trying to avoid God's command to go to Nineveh, a major Assyrian city, and tell its inhabitants to repent. Instead, he boards a ship but it is storm tossed and the sailors throw Jonah into the sea where he is swallowed by a huge fish. Eventually, he reaches dry land and God commands him a second time to go to Nineveh. There, he delivers his message. The people repent and God forgives them.

Jonah, Book of a short book of only four chapters describing Jonah's mission to Nineveh. It is the 5th book in **Trei Asar**, the Twelve Prophets. Jonah is read in the synagogue in the afternoon service of **Yom Kippur**, the Day of Atonement, since its theme is God's readiness to forgive anyone who repents sincerely.

Joseph Hebrew Yosef (*yo-sef*) son of **Jacob** and **Rachel**. Joseph's brothers sold him as a slave. He was taken to Egypt where he rose to a position of great authority and responsibility. Years later, a famine in **Canaan** forced Jacob to send his sons to Egypt to buy food. There, Joseph recognised them although they did not know him. Eventually, Joseph and his brothers were

reconciled and, at Joseph's suggestion, Jacob and the rest of his household settled in Egypt. This paved the way for the Egyptian slavery. Joseph's two sons, Menasseh and Ephraim, became the fathers of the tribes that bore their names. ▶ See also twelve tribes.

Joshua Hebrew Yehoshua (*ye-ho-shu-a*) **Moses'** personal assistant and successor. After Moses died, Joshua led the Israelites across the River Jordan to take possession of the **promised land**. The conquest took seven years, after which Joshua took a further seven years to distribute the land and organise the settlement programme. ▶ See map 2.

Joshua, Book of the first book of the **Neviim**, the prophets. It continues from where **Deuteronomy** ends, charting the career of Joshua and the Israelites and mapping out their conquests. It also lists the areas Joshua did not conquer. The theme of the book is that if the Israelites would be loyal to God and live according to His will, all would go well for them.

Judah Hebrew Yehudah (*ye-hu-dah*) **1)** fourth son of **Jacob** and **Leah**, father of the tribe of Judah; **2)** the tribe of Judah, the dominant southern tribe during the period of the **Judges**; **3)** the southern kingdom (as opposed to Israel) in the time of the divided monarchy. After the return from Babylonian exile in the 6th century BCE, the territory was known as Yehud.

Later, the Romans called it Iudaea (Judea).

Judah Halevi (1075–1141) Jewish philosopher and poet. His most important work, the *Kuzari* (called after the king of the Khazars who converted to Judaism) takes the form of a discussion between a Jew and Christian, Muslim and Aristotelian scholars. Halevi uses the discussion format to demonstrate the superiority of Judaism over the other belief systems. In arguing with the Aristotelian, Halevi's Jewish scholar points out that approaching God through reason is inferior to direct experience of God. His argument against the Christian and Muslim scholars is that Judaism is based on the experience of many thousands of people at **Mount Sinai**, whereas since those religions have no such historical experience, they need Judaism for their own basis. He sees value in Christianity and Islam in spreading Jewish truths throughout the world. However, he insists that they have introduced certain falsehoods which they will come to realise as God's plan unfolds.

Judah the Prince (late 2nd, early 3rd century CE) also called the Patriarch; compiler of the **Mishnah**, known in the **Talmud** simply as 'Rabbi' – the master. Rabbi Judah exercised tremendous authority over the Jews of Israel and was on good terms with the Roman administration. Nonetheless he detested Romans as the destroyers of the **Temple**. His greatest achievement was the compilation of the **Mishnah**, which was completed after his death.

Judenfrage (*yu-den-fra-ge*) German, the Jewish Question. The Question emerged in the late 18th century in discussions about the position of Jews in a modern state. In its basic form, the Question was 'can Jews be loyal citizens of the country in which they reside and keep all its laws if, at the same time, they have ties of loyalty to Jews in other countries and live by their own laws?' ▶ See also **Emancipation, Final Solution, Herzl.**

Judenrein (*yu-den-rine*) German 'free (lit. clean) of Jews', a term used by the Nazis to refer to areas from which Jews had been, or were expected to be, eliminated. ▶ See **Final Solution, Shoah.**

Judenstaat, Der the Jewish State, a short book and manifesto of **Zionism** published by Theodor Herzl in 1896. In it, he refers to the 'Jewish Question' (▶ see **Judenfrage**) and argues that the hostility of the nations and the Jewish people's own will to remain a separate group make it impossible for the question to be resolved by Jews continuing to live among the nations. The only answer lay in an independent Jewish state. He recommended setting up a Society of Jews to handle the project's legal and administrative affairs and a Jewish Company to take care of the finance and to acquire land either in **Palestine** or Argentina. *Der Judenstaat* was rejected by **Orthodox** Jews because it made no provision for Judaism and by assimilated Jews because they felt at home in Europe. However, most of the **Hovovei Zion** hailed it enthusiastically and turned to Herzl for leadership.

Judges Hebrew Shofetim (*sho-fe-tim*) men, many of them prophets, who led the Israelites between the late 14th and early 10th centuries BCE. They came from different tribes and often rose to prominence when the spirit of God came upon them. In spite of this, when an enemy attacked, they could only rally those tribes who were actually threatened.

When the Philistines aimed at total conquest (unlike other hostile neighbours who merely came to plunder) the Israelites felt they needed stronger leadership than the Judges could give and demanded a king. ▶ See **Samuel**.

Judges, Book of the 2nd book of the **Neviim**, the Prophets. Judges takes up the history of the Israelite tribes from the death of **Joshua** and outlines the careers of the judges (see previous entry). The book ends describing a civil war in which the tribe of Benjamin was almost wiped out. ▶ See **Av**.

K

Kabbalah (*ka-ba-lah*) lit. that which is received, a term used for Jewish mysticism. Kabbalah deals with how God created the universe out of nothing, how He sustains its existence, the nature of the soul and the effects of human actions on the upper worlds. The most important kabbalistic work is the **Zohar**, the Book of Splendour, published in the 14th century but containing

teachings going back more than a thousand years earlier. In the past, very few people studied kabbalah as one had to be mature, learned and pious before one was considered fit to do so. Rabbi Israel **Baal Shem Tov** (1698–1760) made it the basis of his philosophy, called **hasidut** and in this form it was taught to a wider audience. Today, there are kabbalistic books in English and societies where kabbalah is studied. These usually bear little relationship to the real thing.

Kaddish (*ka-dish*) sanctification, a declaration of God's praise recited at certain points during communal prayers, ie when a service is held with a **minyan** (at least ten adult males).

Kaddish yatom (*ka-dish ya-tom*) a declaration of God's praise recited by mourners – sometimes mistakenly thought of as a prayer for the dead. It is a statement that, even though God has taken their loved one, they accept His decision and continue to glorify Him. ▶ See also **avelut, sheloshim, shivah, yarzheit.**

Kahan, Rabbi Yisrael Meir

(1838–1933) foremost halakhic authority of the early 20th century, known as the Chafetz Chaim (he who desires life) after the title of one of his major works. He established a **yeshivah** (Talmudic academy), in Radin, Poland, where he devoted himself to the intellectual and moral development of his students. He is best known for his writings on the **halakhic** and moral issues involved in slanderous talk. Rabbi Kahan was one of the first East European rabbis to concern himself with the education of girls and supported Sarah **Scheneirer** in the development of her school system by mapping out an educational programme for young women. He believed fervently in the coming of the **messiah** and supported a group of **cohanim** (priests, like himself) who studied the laws relating to **Temple** ritual so that they would be ready as soon as the messiah appeared. Rabbi Kahan was one of the founding members of **Agudat Yisrael.**

Kaparot (*ka-pa-rot*) forgivenesses (singular kaparah). On the eve of **Yom Kippur**, the Day of Atonement, Jews rise early to perform a ceremony during which they pray for forgiveness. In some communities, a live chicken is held during the ceremony to call to mind the sacrifices in the ancient **Temple**. It is afterwards slaughtered and its meat given to the poor for the Yom Kippur meal.

Karaites from the Hebrew *kara*, that which is read, Jews who accept the authority of the **Written Torah** but not the **Oral Torah**. The sect emerged during the 7th century CE. Although they rely solely on the written text of the Torah, their leaders are at liberty to interpret it as they wish, without any reference to a tradition. Before World War II, there were about 12,000 Karaites in the world. Today, there are small Karaite communities in Israel where they have their own synagogues and religious courts.

Kashrut (*kash-rut*) the state of being **kosher.** ▶ See **kosher** for details.

Kavannah (*ka-va-nah*) lit. concentration, devotion; the thought or intention behind the performance of the commandments. The term is often used in connection with prayer, where it can refer to different levels of concentration ranging from merely being aware that one is standing before God, to concentrating on the meaning of what one is saying, to being totally absorbed in God's presence. ▶ See also **Baal Shem Tov, devekut.**

Kedoshim (*ke-dosh-im*) lit. holy ones; a term used for Jewish martyrs.

Ketubah (*ke-too-bah*) a marriage document, plural ketubot (*ke-tu-bot*). Traditionally, ketubot are written in **Aramaic**, though today many have a modern language translation. The ketubah is a statement of the husband's undertaking to feed, clothe and care for his wife and to make her his number one priority – 'even if I have to sell the coat on my back'. The ketubah remains the wife's property throughout the marriage.

Ketuvim (*ke-too-vim*) the Holy Writings – **Psalms, Proverbs, Job, Song of Songs, Ruth, Lamentations, Ecclesiastes, Esther, Daniel, Ezra, Nehemiah** and **Chronicles**. These books form the third part of the **Tenakh**, the Jewish Bible. It is a varied collection; details of each book are given under its English name. Jews regard these books as holy, but not as sacred as the **Torah**.

Kibbutz (*ki-butz*) a collective settlement in Israel, ie one where property is owned collectively rather than individually, plural kibbutzim (*ki-bu-tzim*); the opposite of a **moshav**. In the early kibbutzim, children were often raised collectively, meeting their parents at regular times; others permitted some expression of individual taste, eg in room decoration. Today, many kibbutzim allow for much more individuality.

Kiddush (*ki-dush*) lit. sanctification, a ceremony performed at the beginning of Sabbath and festival meals. It comprises a blessing said over a cup of wine, praising God for blessing the Jewish people with His holy days.

Kiddush hashem (*ki-dush ha-shem*) lit. sanctifying God's name, ie giving up one's life rather than transgress one of God's commandments – so called because it demonstrates that dying in order to remain loyal to God is preferable to living in disloyalty. Jews are expected to sacrifice their lives rather than publicly commit one of the three cardinal sins – murder, adultery or idolatry. In a time of persecution, they are expected to choose kiddush hashem rather than violate other commandments too.

Kiddush levanah (*ki-dush le-va-nah*) sanctification on seeing the moon, a short service recited during the first half of the month while the moon is waxing. It is always said out of doors in the moonlight. In this prayer, Jews praise God for maintaining the regular movements of the cosmos.

Kiddushin (*ki-du-shin*) lit. sanctification; a term used to mean becoming married. The term reflects the importance of marriage in Jewish life. It also expresses the belief that men and women entering into marriage complete each other's personality growth, for through marriage they become able to fulfil their duties to people and to God as complete human beings. ▶ See also **erusin, nisuin.**

Kings, Book of Kings begins with the death of King **David**, follows the career of his son Solomon and describes the division into two kingdoms, **Israel** in the north and **Judah** in the south. It outlines the history of these two kingdoms, dealing with the overthrow of Israel by Assyria and the deportation of its population in 722 BCE, and concludes with the defeat of Judah and the destruction of the first **Temple** by the Babylonians in 586 BCE. Due to its length, it was later found convenient to divide it into two books, known as I Kings and II Kings.

Kinot (*ki-not*) dirges, poems of lament, singular kinah (*ki-nah*). Kinot were composed mainly during the Middle Ages to mourn the destruction of Jewish communities. More recently, kinot have been written in memory of those Jews who perished in the **Holocaust.**

They are said on **Tishah b'Av**, the 9th of Av.

Kippah (*ki-pah*) small cap worn by Jewish males as a mark of respect for God (Jewish women are only required to cover their hair after they are married). Also called **kuppel** or **yarmulka.**

The **kippah** worn by Jewish males.

Kislev (*kis-lev*) 9th month of the Jewish year. The 25th Kislev is the beginning of Hanukah, an eight day celebration marking the rededication of the Temple after its defilement by idolatrous worship.

Kittel (*ki-tle*) Yiddish, a white garment, rather like a smock, worn by Jewish men on **Yom Kippur**, the Day of Atonement. It symbolises the verse, 'If your sins should be as red as scarlet, I will make them as white as snow' (Isaiah 1:18). In some communities, the kittel is also worn at the **seder**, the Passover meal.

Knesset (*k-ne-set*) lit. assembly, the Israeli parliament. The Knesset consists of 120 democratically elected members representing several parties.

Kodashim (*ko-da-shim*) lit. holy things, the fifth section (called Order) of the **Mishnah**. Kodashim deals with **Temple** ritual in general; one volume gives a description of the building, including its dimensions.

Kohelet (*ko-he-let*) ▶ see **Ecclesiastes**.

Kollel (*ko-lel*) an advanced Jewish academy of higher standard than a **yeshivah**, plural kollelim (*kol-le-lim*). The students in a kollel are usually adults who continue studying **Talmud** and **Halachah** (Jewish law) after they are married. Kollel graduates usually become rabbis, lecturers in yeshivot (Talmudic colleges) or **dayanim**, rabbinic judges.

Kol Nidrei (*kol nid-rey*) a declaration annulling vows said at the beginning of the **Yom Kippur**, Day of Atonement, service – called after its opening words, *kol nidrei ve'esarei...* 'all vows and oaths...'. Kol nidrei originated at the time of the Visigoth persecutions, becoming particularly important during the Spanish Inquisition. At that time, Jews were forced to become Christians but many lived secretly as Jews (▶ see **Marranos**). Each year, before they renewed their oaths of allegiance to the Church, they would gather to declare them null and void. It is said today to remind Jews of

their ancestors' self-sacrifice for Judaism.

Kook, Rabbi Avraham Yitzchak (1865–1935) first **Ashkenazi Chief Rabbi** of **Palestine**. Rabbi Kook was a deeply religious man who upheld the Zionist ideal. He tried to win over both those rabbis who opposed **Zionism** as well as those Zionists who were hostile to Judaism. He believed that the Jews' return to the Holy Land was the **athalta digeulta**, the beginning of the messianic age, and that the establishment of the Chief Rabbinate in 1921 was the first step towards a **Sanhedrin**, a supreme rabbinic council. Rabbi Kook had a deep love for all the Jewish people, even those who cried out against him for associating with secularists. He taught that **secular** Jews who build the Holy Land are doing God's work without realising it. He consistently upheld what he regarded as true Jewish values, criticising both those who were immersed in materialism and those who observed the commandments carefully but ignored social issues. For Rabbi Kook, the Jewish destiny was bound up with the Holy Land; the return to Palestine was not due to the Zionists choosing the Land of Israel but was the unfolding of God's plan.

Korach (*ko-rach*) a cousin of Moses who led a rebellion against him. His complaint was that since all the people of Israel are holy, it was wrong of Moses to put himself above anyone else and make his brother high priest (Numbers 16:3). Two hundred and fifty senior Israelites supported him. Moses tried pointing out that it was God who had made the appointments but it proved impossible to reason with Korach and his followers since their quarrel was simply a bid for power. Finally, an earthquake that swallowed Korach and his followers demonstrated that Moses and Aaron had been chosen by God.

Korban Pesach (*kor-ban Pe-sach*) the **Passover** sacrifice. When the **Temple** stood, a young sheep or goat would be brought as an offering; parts of it would be offered on the altar, the rest was roasted over an open fire and eaten in memory of the departure from Egypt (Exodus 12:9). Today it is represented by a burnt bone on the **seder plate** and the afikomen, the last piece of **matzah** eaten after the Passover meal. ▶ See also **zeroa**.

Kosher (*ka-sher*) often pronounced *Ko-sher* by **Ashkenazim**, lit. right, correct. **1)** correct to eat, ie the right kind of food for Jews to eat, the opposite of **treifah**. The basic requirements of kosher food are laid down in Leviticus chapter 11; (i) only animals that chew cud and

have completely parted hooves may be kosher, (ii) all birds, except those listed in the chapter are kosher (though in practice, Jews normally eat only chicken, duck and turkey, (iii) only fish that have fins and scales are kosher. In addition, animals must be killed by the **shechitah** method and their blood removed (Leviticus 3:17); Jews are not permitted to eat or prepare meat and dairy foods at the same meal. ▶ See also **hechsher. 2)** correct for use, the opposite of **pasul**. When used in this context, kosher refers specifically to ritual objects; for example, a **Torah scroll** can be kosher (fit for use) or pasul (unfit for use).

Kotel ▶ see **Hakotel Hamaaravi**.

Kuppel (*ku-ple*) ▶ see **kippah**.

Kvatter (*kva-ter*) Yiddish, the people who carry a baby boy to and from his circumcision, usually a husband and wife. The wife takes the baby from his mother and carries him to the room where the men are gathered. There she hands him to her husband who carries the child to his father. After the circumcision, the child is carried back the same way and given to his mother for feeding.

Lag ba'Omer (*lag ba-O-mer*) the 33rd day of the Omer, the period between **Pesach** and **Shavuot**. Lag is a word formed from the Hebrew letters lamed (with the sound l) and gimel (with the sound g), these representing the numbers 30 and 3 respectively (see **gematria**). Lag ba'Omer is celebrated as a semi-festive day in memory of a plague that broke out some time before the **Bar Kokhba** revolt in 132 CE that almost wiped out the nation's leadership. On Lag ba'Omer no-one died and the plague began to abate. Jews mark Lag ba'Omer as a symbol of survival. There are no set celebrations, but children are usually taken on outings.

Ladino a Jewish dialect of Spanish. After the Jews were expelled from Spain in 1492, it became the common language of Jews of Spanish origin, although the further they migrated from Spain the more their Ladino became mixed with the words and usages of other languages (compare **Yiddish**). The Bible was translated into Ladino in the 13th century.

Lamdan (*lam-dan*) a scholar, in particular one well versed in **Talmud** and **halakhic** literature. Becoming a lamdan is the ideal nurtured in the **yeshivot**, Talmudic academies.

Lamentations, Book of Hebrew Echah (*e-chah*), 'how'; called after the opening phrase, 'How the city [ie Jerusalem] sits all alone'. It is one of the **Chamesh Megillot**, the Five Scrolls, and is a lament over the destruction of **Jerusalem** and the first **Temple** in descriptive and poetic language. According to the **Talmud**, it was written by **Jeremiah**. Lamentations is read in the synagogue on **Tishah b'Av**, the Fast of Av.

Leah first of **Jacob's** four wives and one of the **matriarchs**, mothers of the Jewish people. Leah had six sons, Reuven, Shimon, Levi, Yehudah, Yissachar and Zevulun and a daughter Dinah (Genesis 29:32–30:21). Leah was buried with Jacob in the Cave of Machpelah in Hebron. ▶ See **mearat hamachpelah, twelve tribes**.

Leshon hakodesh (*le-shon ha-ko-desh*) lit. the tongue of holiness or the holy tongue ie the **Hebrew** language. Hebrew is so called because it is the language in which God gave the **Torah** on Mount Sinai. To this day, most Jewish prayers are said in Hebrew.

Leshon hara (*le-shon ha-ra*) lit. the tongue of evil, ie slanderous talk. Jews are forbidden to engage in leshon hara, even when the slander is true. Indeed, slander that is not true is considered even more serious and is referred to by a term of its own – *motzi shem ra*, lit. bringing out a bad name, ie damaging someone's reputation. ▶ See **Kahan**.

Levayah (*le-va-yah*) lit. accompanying ie taking a dead person to his or her final resting place. After a body has been prepared for burial, it will usually be taken to the house where the person lived. Friends and relatives will have gathered there and, sometimes after hearing speeches, will walk with the body as it leaves the house. Some people will accompany it to the cemetery. There, the levayah will continue until the grave side. ▶ See also **avelut, chevra kaddisha, hesped, onen**.

Levi (*le-vi*) **1)** third son of Jacob; **2)** the tribe that descended from Jacob's third son; **3)** an individual member of the tribe of Levi, plural leviim (*le- vi-im*); called Levites in English. The leviim assisted the priests in the Temple and sang in the choir. They possessed no territory in the Holy Land, except for certain specified cities.

Leviticus 3rd book of the Bible, so called because it deals largely with **Temple** ritual which was conducted by the Tribe of **Levi**; called **Vayikra** in Hebrew.

Liberal movement a movement founded by Claude **Montefiore** who found the Judaism of the **Reform Movement** too demanding. The movement teaches that the Torah was not given by direct revelation and maintains that keeping the commandments is optional, depending on what each individual feels he or she ought to observe (▶ see **enlightened consciousness**). Liberals regard anyone brought up as Jewish to be a Jew whatever their parentage, just as they regard a Jew brought up in another faith to be a non-Jew. Some Liberals do not believe in the immortality of the soul, thinking of immortality as simply being remembered after one's death.

Lilienblum, Moshe Leib (1843– 1910) leader of **Hibat Zion**, an accomplished **Talmudic** scholar who abandoned religion. He believed that **anti-semitism** could not be eradicated, neither by Jews adapting their lifestyle to that of the surrounding culture nor by legal emancipation. It would continue as long as Jews lived among other nations, whose own nationalist ideals had no place for them. The solution lay in establishing a Jewish homeland in **Palestine**, where Jews would not be foreigners. He believed that the aim of Hibat Zion should be to buy land in Palestine and set up a Jewish government over it. ▶ See also **autoemancipation, Pinsker**.

Lipkin, Rabbi Yisrael of Salant (1810–1883) founder of the

Musar Movement. As a teacher, Rabbi Lipkin was deeply concerned about people's moral development. He first began preaching musar (Jewish religious ethics) in his sermons and subsequently opened a musar shteibel (room for reflection) in Vilna. Although people flocked to hear him speak, there was little enthusiasm for his musar rooms. He founded a **yeshivah**, Talmudic academy, in Kovno and began teaching musar to his students, insisting that they also pay attention to their appearance. Other leading rabbis opposed the teaching of musar, claiming that it wasted students' time when they could be engaged in academic studies. They began changing their minds when they saw the kind of students Rabbi Lipkin was producing.

Lulav (*lu-lav*) palm branch, one of the arbaat **haminim**, the four plant species used during prayers on **Sukkot**. The lulav is always a young branch, whose long, pointed leaves have not yet opened up to form the characteristic palm branch shape.

M

Mearat hamachpelah (*me-a-rat ha-mach-pe-lah*) lit. double cave, a cave in Hebron that **Abraham** bought as a family tomb when his wife, **Sarah**, died (Genesis 23: 16–18). **Isaac** and **Rebekkah** and **Jacob** and **Leah** were later buried there. So, according to tradition, were Adam and Eve. Today, mearat hamachpelah is a holy site for Jews and Muslims (who also claim descent from Abraham).

Maariv (*ma-a-riv*) another name for the evening prayer, ▶ see **arvit**.

Maccabean revolt a Jewish revolt against the Syrian-Greek king, **Antiochus** IV. The Holy Land was part of the Seleucid Empire, which Antiochus ruled. He issued a number of decrees aimed at abolishing the Jewish religion. Jews who resisted him were tortured and killed. In 168 BCE, the Jews rose in armed revolt and, after three years fighting, drove Antiochus' armies out. It is known as the Maccabean revolt since it was led by Judah the Maccabee (Hebrew for hammer). ▶ See also **Hanukah**.

Machatzit hashekel (*ma-cha-tzit ha-she-kel*) half a shekel, the Temple tax ie money collected from Jews all over the world in ancient times and used for communal offerings and the upkeep of the Temple. When the second Temple was destroyed, the Romans seized the tax for their own use. Today, a symbolic half-shekel is given on the Fast of Esther. It often goes towards the running costs of the synagogue.

Machzor (*mach-zor*) prayer book for festivals, plural machzorim (*mach-zo-rim*), so called because it follows the machzor, the cycle of the year. Most machzorim contain translations and directions for following the service. ▶ See **siddur**.

Magen David (*ma-gen da-vid*) lit. shield of **David**, a six pointed star. No-one knows the origin of this design nor why it came to be associated with David, though there are several theories. However, it has come to be a symbol of Judaism. Today, a blue Magen David is at the centre of the flag of **Israel**.

Magen David Adom (*ma-gen da-vid a-dom*) lit. red shield of David; the Israeli ambulance service, which

has as its symbol a red Magen David.

Maggid (*ma-gid*) **1)** as a verb, telling, the main part of the **seder**, the Passover meal, when Jews recount their ancestors' departure from Egyptian slavery; **2)** as a noun, a teller, ie a preacher, a term used in Eastern Europe for rabbis who delivered sermons on moral themes in the synagogue. Rabbi Yisrael **Baal Shem Tov** started his career as a maggid, bringing hope to thousands. ▶ See **Hasidic movement** and next entry.

Maggid of Mezritch Rabbi Dov Baer, successor to Rabbi Yisrael **Baal Shem Tov** and leader of the **Hasidic** movement 1760–1772. Whereas Rabbi Yisrael had created a popular movement, Rabbi Dov Baer saw that it would soon become too large to be held together by one man and concentrated his efforts on preparing his most able students for leadership. This actually ensured the movement's survival for, within a few years of Rabbi Dov Baer's death, several local centres had been established in various parts of Eastern Europe, each with its own leader. ▶ See also **Rebbe**.

Maimonides Rabbi Moshe ben Maimon (1135–1204), Jewish philosopher and one of the major **halakhic** authorities. Although he wrote a commentary on the **Mishnah**, a book explaining the commandments and **responsa**, his most influential halakhic work was the **Mishneh Torah**, a **code** of Jewish law. He wrote it, as he explains in his introduction, 'so that a person may read the **Written Torah** first and then read this and know the entire **Oral Torah** without having to consult another book'. The Mishneh Torah was the first code to appear with the halakhot classified under clear subject headings (compare **Saadia Gaon**). Indeed, those who opposed it did so on the grounds that it was so clear that it might make **Talmud** study unnecessary. Maimonides' principal philosophical work was the *Guide for the Perplexed*, written to help Jews whose study of philosophy had left them confused about the meaning of the many figurative statements in the Torah. In this work he discusses the question of how God reveals Himself to the **prophets**, the nature of evil and the reason for the commandments. His in-depth analysis of these and other themes occupied Jewish thinkers for generations. His help was sought by Jewish communities who were suffering persecution. When the **Yemenite** Jews were given the choice of accepting Islam or death, he gave them renewed hope and used his influence with the Sultan of Egypt (whose personal physician he was) to help them.

Malachi (*ma-la-chi*) the last of the **prophets**. Malachi lived in the early 5th century BCE and addressed the problems of the newly formed community of Jerusalem, following the return from **Babylonian exile**. People had expected the rebuilding

of the **Temple** to be the start of a glorious new age. They were disappointed that this had not happened and had become lax in their religious observances. Some had taken heathen wives. Malachi tried to raise standards of observance, teaching that religious practices needed sincerity and enthusiasm because they were spiritual acts. Like the earlier prophets, Malachi cried out against those who oppressed the underprivileged.

Malachi, Book of the 12th and last book of **Trei Asar**, the Twelve Prophets. The book contains six speeches delivered by Malachi. Their themes are: (i) God's love for the Jewish people; (ii) the importance of Temple offerings; (iii) a speech against **out-marriage**; (iv) a justification of God's justice; (v) the importance of tithes; (vi) an assurance that the righteous will prosper.

Mamzer (*mam-zer*) a child born of a woman who commits adultery, plural mamzerim (*mam-ze-rim*). The term is sometimes taken to mean a child whose parents are not married. This is incorrect. Mamzerim, through no fault of their own, may not marry into the Jewish community; although a mamzer may marry another mamzer or a convert to Judaism (a proselyte).

Mamzerut (*mam-ze-rut*) condition of being a **mamzer**.

Mandate the period of British administration of **Palestine**, 1923–1948; so called because it was mandated, ie authorised, by the League of Nations. Relations between the Jews of Palestine and the Mandate authorities were never very good. However, they soured at the end of World War II when there was a sudden and urgent need to resettle thousands of **Holocaust** survivors and Britain placed severe restrictions on Jewish immigration – even turning back ships bringing survivors from Displaced Persons-Camps. Jewish groups began attacking British military targets in Palestine, eventually forcing Britain to give up the Mandate. The day after the last British troops left, the Jews declared the State of Israel.

Maror (*ma-ror*) bitter herb eaten at the **seder**, the Passover meal to call to mind the bitterness of the Israelites' slavery. Various vegetables are in use. However, the recommended bitter herb is lettuce – not that its leaves are bitter, but because it grows from a bitter stalk. The crisp, tender leaves growing out of a bitter stalk symbolise the Israelites' freedom emerging from bitter slavery.

Marrano Spanish, swine, a term of contempt used by the Spanish and Portuguese to refer to the Jews of those countries who converted to Christianity in the 14th–16th centuries. Converting to avoid persecution, many lived outwardly as Christians while practising

Judaism in secret. Native Spanish Christians generally doubted the sincerity of the 'New Christians' (often with good reason) and subjected them to all sorts of legal disabilities.

Massada a hilltop fortress near the southern tip of the Dead Sea. It was built by King Herod the Great as a refuge to which he could flee in time of trouble. It has become famous as the **Zealots** last stand, where over a thousand men, women and children held out against the Romans for three years after the fall of Jerusalem in 70 CE. When defeat became imminent, the men killed their families and then themselves rather than fall into the Romans' hands, where they knew they would be tortured and enslaved.

Mashiach (*ma-shi-ach*) lit. anointed one, the messiah, a future leader – a man of exceptional scholarship, piety and charisma – who is expected to lead all Jews to the **Holy Land**, rebuild the **Temple** and usher in an age of universal peace when all humankind will worship the one true God. Over the centuries, several people have claimed to be the mashiach or had their followers make that claim for them. ▶ See **Shabbatai Zevi**.

Maskil (*mas-kil*) a follower of **Haskalah**, plural maskilim (*mas-ki-lim*), a movement that began in the late 18th century and aimed to integrate Jews into the **secular** world. ▶ See **Mendelssohn**.

Masorti Movement the British equivalent of the **Conservative Movement**. The seeds of Masorti were sown in 1964 when Dr. Louis Jacobs, formerly rabbi of an **Orthodox** synagogue, was appointed minister of an independent congregation following the **Chief Rabbi's** refusal to allow him to continue in office. From 1974, a small number of independent congregations, all looking to Dr. Jacobs as their spiritual head, banded together to form the Masorti Movement. Masorti claims to offer an '**Orthodox** style' Judaism. However, it teaches that God did not give the whole of the Torah at Mount Sinai and has moved away from the traditional pattern; some of its synagogues have mixed seating and it accepts as ministers people trained in **Reform** institutions. Neither Masorti marriages nor conversions are recognised by the Orthodox authorities. ▶ See also **Frankel**.

Matzah (*ma-tzah*) a mixture of flour and water baked quickly to form thin, wafer-like bread; called unleavened bread since the dough does not rise by the action of yeast; plural matzot (*ma-tzot*). Matzah was the food given to the Israelites while they were slaves in Egypt; it was also the bread they baked in the sun as they marched out to freedom. Jews eat matzah during Passover to commemorate God taking their ancestors out of slavery. ▶ See also **Moses, Pesach, Pharaoh.**

Matriarchs the mothers of the Jewish people, **Sarah, Rebekah, Rachel** and **Leah**. Jacob's other wives, Bilhah and Zilpah, are not usually included, although their sons became the fathers of four of the **twelve tribes**. Sarah, Rebekah and Leah are buried in the **Mearat Hamachpelah** in Hebron. Rachel, who died in childbirth, was buried by the roadside on the way to Bethlehem.

Megillah (*me-gi-lah*) lit. scroll, usually taken to refer to the **Book of Esther**. ▶ See also **Chamesh Megillot, Esther**.

Meir, Rabbi (2nd century CE) student of Rabbi **Akiva** and one of the foremost rabbinic leaders in the period following the **Bar Kokhba** revolt of 132–135. During those years, he became a calming influence, teaching a moderate attitude toward Rome (which he actually detested). He continued Rabbi Akiva's task of systematising the **halakhah** (Jewish law), and much of his work was subsequently

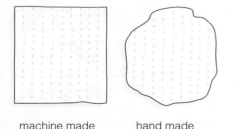

machine made   hand made

Two types of **matzah**.

incorporated into the **Mishnah**. He was revered as a holy man and the kehilla kaddisha, a community of scholars whose lives were based on **Torah** study, prayer and work, looked to him as their mentor. He tried to popularise Torah teachings by using simple parables and is said to have made up 300 'fox stories'.

Melachah (*me-la-chah*) lit. work, job, task, plural melachot (*me-la-chot*). With regard to Sabbath observance, a melachah is one of the 39 types of work that were needed for building the **mishkan**, the portable Temple the Israelites constructed in the desert. They were forbidden to make any part of it on the Sabbath day and from this is derived the principle that those 39 categories of work are forbidden on the Sabbath. They are:

1 ploughing	23 sewing
2 sowing	24 tearing
3 reaping	25 trapping
4 sheaf making	26 slaughtering
5 threshing	27 skinning
6 winnowing	28 tanning
7 selecting	29 scraping pelts
8 sifting	30 marking out
9 kneading	31 cutting to shape
10 baking	32 writing
11 sheep shearing	33 erasing
12 bleaching	34 building
13 combing raw	35 demolishing
materials	36 lighting a fire
14 dyeing	37 putting out a fire
15 spinning	38 finishing a new
16-19 various weaving	article
operations	39 carrying from a
20 separating into	private to a
threads	public area and
21 tying a knot	vice versa
22 untying a knot	

Wherever the **Torah** forbids 'work' on the Sabbath, it refers to these 39 categories.

Melechet avodah (*me-le-chet a-vo-dah*) lit. productive work, a term used for any **melachah**, form of work forbidden on the Sabbath, which is not connected with preparing food. On Sabbath, every melachah is forbidden; on festivals, when food may be prepared, only those tasks classed as melechet avodah are forbidden.

Mendelssohn, Moses

(1729–1786) founder of **Haskalah**, a movement for bringing Jewish life in line with contemporary **secular** society. Young Mendelssohn received a traditional education and taught himself Latin, Greek and modern languages. Living in Berlin, he gained a formidable reputation as a philosopher and became a fashionable figure in the salons where the intellectuals of the day would gather. He was often called upon to help Jewish communities who were having difficulties with the authorities. Mendelssohn believed that the Jews' civic status should be improved but maintained that the Jews themselves had to make changes if people were to accept them. He encouraged Jews to learn trades and take up agriculture, to dress like the people among whom they lived and to learn to speak their language. However, it was the man himself rather than his beliefs that set the movement for **secularisation** in motion. Other Jews saw the esteem in which he was held in the non-Jewish world and wanted to achieve the same.

The menorah being taken from the Temple.

Menorah (*me-no-rah*) lit. lamp, a seven-branched oil lamp made of solid gold that originally stood in the **mishkan**, the portable temple the Israelites built in the desert, and subsequently in the **Temple**. It burned olive oil and the priests lit it each day. The menorah stood near

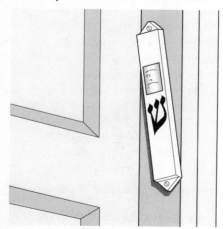

A **mezuzah** on the door post of a Jewish house.

the entrance to the **Holy of Holies** and the light nearest to it was never permitted to go out. After the persecutions of **Antiochus** IV (175–163 BCE) when the Jews regained possession of the Temple, they relit the menorah with the small amount of oil they found and the menorah became the central focus of the miracle of **Hanukah**. ▶ See also **hanukiah, ner tamid.**

Messiah ▶ see **Mashiach.**

Mezuzah (*me-zu-zah*) lit. door post; a small parchment scroll containing the first two paragraphs of the **Shema**, plural mezuzot (*me-zu-zot*). In response to the command 'you shall write them on the door posts of your house' (Deuteronomy 6:9), a mezuzah is fixed to the door frame of every room except the bathroom and toilet – these being considered inappropriate sites for a sacred object. Before fixing the mezuzah in position, it is placed inside a cover (usually metal, wood or plastic) to protect it from damp and dust. This has led some people to think that the case is the mezuzah. This is incorrect.

Micah (*mee-chah*) a prophet of the late 8th century BCE, a contemporary of **Isaiah**. Micah was mainly concerned with the moral degeneration of his time. Addressing the people of **Judah**, he cried out against the powerful landowners who found ways of seizing ever more land, corrupt judges who took bribes and the rulers who committed acts of violence to get their own way. He also denounced the 'false prophets' who took payment for telling people whatever they wanted to hear.

Micah, Book of the 6th book of **Trei Asar**, the Twelve Prophets. The book is arranged in three parts. Chapters 1–3 contain a speech against the corrupt leaders and their acts of violence, chapters 4–5 describe the **messianic** future when all nations will come to Mount Zion to hear the words of God and chapters 6–7 explain how God has kept His part of the covenant while the people of Israel have broken theirs.

Midrash (*mid-rash*) a method of teaching in which important lessons are communicated as short stories, plural midrashim (*mid-ra-shim*). These stories might be taken or adapted from real life events; they might simply be figurative. They often contain a good deal of factual material which might not be known from other sources. Midrash was often used to explain verses in the **Torah**. The earliest midrashim were written down in the 1st century BCE, the latest date from the 10th century.

Migrash (*mig-rash*) an open space, 1000 **cubits** wide, that surrounded towns in ancient Israel (Numbers 35:4). The migrash was neither available for planting crops, grazing animals nor setting up a business. It simply provided a light airy surround for the benefit of the town dwellers. It also limited the size of towns since no-one was permitted to build out onto the migrash.

Mikveh (*mik-veh*) a pool of natural water; plural mikvaot (*mik-va-ot*).

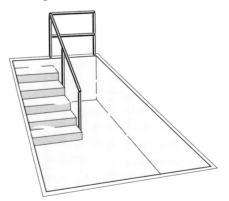

A **mikveh** is a special pool for women.

There are two kinds of mikveh; (i) those where people immerse themselves. These contain clean,

heated tap water joined to a tank of natural water. They are used mainly by women for purification after menstruation or childbirth. Adjoining the pool area are bathrooms where women prepare for their immersion. They are normally built away from the public view for reasons of modesty. There are also mikvaot for men.
(ii) Mikvaot where utensils are immersed. They are usually tanks where rain water has collected. These are found outside some synagogues. ▶ See also **nidah, tevillah, tevillat kelim.**

Milah (*mee-lah*) surgical removal of the foreskin, the flap of skin that overhangs the tip of the penis. It is carried out as a sign of the covenant between Jews and God. ▶ See **brit milah.**

Milchemet mitzvah (*mil-che-met mitz-vah*) obligatory war, a war undertaken either in response to a command from God (eg **Joshua's** wars to conquer **Canaan**) or a war fought in self defence (which includes preventing an attack).

Milchemet reshut (*mil-che-met re-shoot*) optional war, a war fought with the consent of the **Sanhedrin**, the supreme Jewish council; usually only undertaken when all other means of achieving peace have been tried and have failed.

Minchah (*Min-chah*) the afternoon service. Minchah consists of a

reading of Psalm 145, the **Shemoneh Esrei**, the prayer for one's needs, a prayer for forgiveness and **Alenu**, the concluding prayer. On Sabbaths and fast days, minchah includes a public **Torah** reading.

Minyan (*min-yan*) lit. number, ie ten adult Jewish males, this being the minimum number required for certain communal prayers and public **Torah** readings.

Miriam (*mir-yam*) **Moses'** sister. She was several years older than Moses. After Moses was born, and his mother could no longer hide him to avoid **Pharaoh's** decree of drowning male children, she placed him in a basket in the Nile. Miriam watched over it and, when Pharaoh's daughter came to bathe and discovered him, she took advantage of the situation by offering to bring an Israelite woman to nurse the baby (Exodus 2:7). She then called Moses' own mother. By doing so, she ensured that Moses would know he was an Israelite, although he would be growing up in the Egyptian royal court as a son to Pharaoh's daughter. After they left Egypt, when Moses led the Israelite men in a victory song at the Red Sea, Miriam led the women (Exodus 15:21).

Mishkan (*mish-can*) lit. resting place, the portable temple the Israelites constructed in the desert. It was made of posts, boards, curtains and ropes (Exodus, chapter 26) and could be assembled and dismantled easily whenever they encamped or set off to a new site.

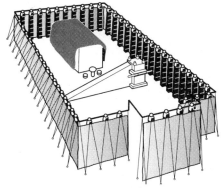

Mishkan – the portable temple constructed by the Israelites in the desert.

Mishnah (*mish-nah*) lit. repetition, the written version of the **Oral Torah** compiled by Rabbi **Judah the Prince** around the year 200 CE. It comprises six divisions (called Orders) and runs into 63 volumes. ► See **Zeraim, Moed, Nashim, Nezikin, Kodashim,Toharot** and individual entries for details. It was known as the Mishnah (repetition) since people repeated it until they knew it by heart.

Mishneh Torah (*mish-neh To-rah*) lit. repetition of the Torah. **1)** Another name for **Devarim**, the Book of **Deuteronomy**, so called because it repeats and expands on some of the commandments mentioned in the earlier books of the **Torah. 2)** A code of Jewish law written by **Maimonides**, Rabbi Moshe ben Maimon, completed in 1190. Maimonides was the first to break with the order of the **Talmud** and arrange the topics in his code

under a logical sequence of subject headings. ► See **codes**.

Mishpatim (*mish-pa-tim*) lit. judgements, commandments in the **Torah** which are common to all societies in some form and which we would have kept even if the Torah had not mentioned them. Examples of mishpatim are the laws forbidding murder (Exodus 20:13) and stealing (Leviticus 19:11). ► See also **chukim, edot**.

Mitnagdim (*mit-nag-dim*) lit. opponents, those who opposed the **Hasidic movement**. Mitnagdim were found mainly among the Jews of Lithuania, where Jewish life centred firmly on **Torah** study. They objected to the fact that the Hasidim did not always keep strictly to the times of prayer as well as to their stress on joy and enthusiasm, fearing that such things would weaken commitment to Torah study. ► See also **Elijah of Vilna**.

Mitzvah (*mitz-vah*) lit. commandment, plural mitzvot (*mitz-vot*). There are 613 mitzvot in the **Torah**, 248 positive commandments (ie things Jews are expected to do) and 365 negative ones (things Jews are expected not to do). For Jews, living by the commandments is fulfilling their part of the **covenant** and is essential to their relationship with God. They see the mitzvot as establishing the framework of a disciplined life, as a means of personality development and, ultimately, as a way of communicating with God.

Mizrahi (*miz-ra-chi*) the religious wing of the World Zionist Organisation, founded in 1902. Mizrahi came into being because of the religious Zionists' struggle to keep cultural affairs out of the hands of secular Jews, its motto being 'The Land of Israel for the People of Israel according to the Torah of Israel'. Mizrahi established a system of religious education in **Palestine** in 1920. Due to the efforts of Mizrahi, the Sabbath is today observed as a public day of rest in **Israel**, the Israeli armed services have **kosher** food and marriage and divorce are administered by the rabbis. ▶ See **Zionism**.

Modeh ani (*mo-deh a-ni*) a short prayer Jews say on waking up each morning, thanking God for restoring their souls and allowing them to awake to a new day; so called after the opening words, modeh ani, 'I give thanks'.

Moed (*mo-ed*) lit. festival the second section (called Order) of the **Mishnah**. Moed deals with Sabbath and festival observance, fast days and other special occasions.

Mohel (*mo-hel*) a person who performs **milah**, circumcision. In Jewish law, a father is obligated to circumcise his own son. However, since most fathers do not know how, they appoint a mohel, a person trained in the surgical technique and licensed by a **bet din** (rabbinical court) or similar body, to do it on their behalf. ▶ See **brit milah**.

Mohilever, Rabbi Samuel (1824–1898) an **Orthodox** leader who, almost uniquely in his day, sought ways of co-operating with irreligious Jews – first with the **maskilim**, those who wanted to **secularise** Jewish life, and later with the **Hibat Zion** movement, when he worked with Dr. Leon **Pinsker** to support Jewish farmers in **Palestine**. As a prominent member of Hibat Zion, Rabbi Mohilever was president of the Kattowitz conference of 1884, setting the tone of future Hibat Zion thought with his speech comparing the renewal of Jewish nationalism with **Ezekiel's** vision of a valley of dry bones (Ezekiel chapter 36). He was adamant that the Hibat Zion programme should be political (ie aimed at Jewish resettlement in Palestine) and that cultural activities be kept in the hands of religious Jews. Later, he became one of the founders of **Mizrahi**. ▶ See also **Ahad Ha'am, Reinnes**.

Monotheism belief in one God. Monotheism is not simply the worship of one god while acknowledging the existence of others (called monolatry) but the belief that there is only one God. For Jews, monotheism also carries the meaning that the one God is the creator and sustainer of all things. This, in turn, means a belief that God is totally different from anything humans can know and he cannot be imagined or depicted in any form.

Montagu, Lilian (Lily) (1873–1963) one of the founders of the **Liberal movement**. Raised in an upper class, orthodox home, Lilian Montagu was appalled by the poverty of the Jewish immigrants, recently arrived from Eastern Europe, and saw how uncomfortable many of them felt about having to work on Sabbaths and festivals. She decided that Judaism ought to be made easier for them. In 1902, together with Claude Montefiore, she formed the Jewish Religious Union, which subsequently became the Union of Liberal and Progressive Synagogues.

Montefiore, Claude (1858–1938) one of the founders of the **Liberal Movement**. Believing that the **Reform** movement had not taken its reforms far enough, he founded the Jewish Religious Union in 1902. Being committed to universalism, he opposed **Zionism** as being too narrow and tried to prevent the **Balfour Declaration** from being issued. His religious outlook centred on his concept of the **enlightened consciousness**, by which he meant studying the sources (ie being enlightened) and, on the basis of that, selecting which parts of Judaism to observe.

Moses Hebrew Mosheh (*mo-sheh*) the lawgiver. Moses was raised in the Egyptian royal court (Exodus 2:1) but fled after killing an Egyptian slave master. Later, God appeared to him and told him to lead the Israelite slaves out of Egypt to a new land. Seven weeks after leaving, Moses received the **Torah** on **Mount Sinai** and began teaching it to the Israelites as he led them through the desert. Forty years later, they arrived at the border of the **promised land**. Moses died in sight of the land, which he blessed but was not permitted to enter. Jews regard Moses as the greatest of the prophets; the only one to have spoken to God 'face to face' (Deuteronomy 34:10).

Moshav (*mo-shav*) a settlement in Israel where people own their houses and other property, plural moshavim (*mo-sha-vim*); the opposite of a **kibbutz**. Most moshavim are farming villages, though some have light industry.

Moshe Rabbenu (*mo-sheh ra-bey-noo*) lit. Moses our teacher, a term of reverence Jews use acknowledging Moses as the one who taught the **Torah** to the Jewish people. ▶ See also **Moses**.

Mount Sinai a mountain in the Sinai Desert where God gave the Torah to the Jewish people (Exodus 19:20); also called Mount Horev (or Horeb). The exact location of Mount Sinai is not known for certain, though the local Bedouins have a tradition about a mountain they call Jebel Musa, the Mountain of **Moses**. Five hundred years after Moses' time, **Elijah** returned to Mount Sinai to receive his final instructions from

God (I Kings 19:8). ► See also **Shavuot**.

Musaf (*mu-saf*) lit. addition, the additional service in the synagogue that follows the public Torah reading at the end of morning prayers of Sabbath, **Rosh Chodesh** (start of new month), and festivals. It is said at the time that the additional sacrifice for these occasions used to be offered in the **Temple**, and so helps keep the memory of the Temple alive.

Musar (*mu-sar*, often pronounced *Mu-sar*) lit. correction, Jewish ethics – so called because it aims to 'correct' people's attitudes and behaviour. Musar entails a careful analysis of the traits Judaism considers undesirable such as pride, anger, greed and laziness, as well as desirable traits such as honesty, justice, compassion and humility. However, the teachings of musar are not simply theoretical; its objective is to actually bring about changes in people. ► See next entry.

Musar Movement a movement that emerged in Lithuania in the mid 19th century aimed at refining people's characters through the study and application of **Musar** (► see previous entry). The movement is largely associated with Rabbi Israel **Lipkin** of Salant who, in 1850, opened a **musar shteibel** (room for contemplation ► see next entry) in Vilna. When this failed to attract people, Rabbi Lipkin turned to the **yeshivot** (Talmudic academies), where he set about developing character building programmes aimed at the youth. Today, the study of musar is an accepted part of the learning programmes of most yeshivot.

Musar shteibel (*mu-sur shtee-bel*) 'ethics room', rooms filled with books on Jewish ethics set up by Rabbi Israel **Lipkin** (1810–1883) in Vilna, where businessmen and other busy people could spend time reflecting on the quality of their lives. ► See also **musar**.

Nachmanides (1194–1270) Rabbi Nachman ben Moshe (known as Ramban) major **Bible** commentator, **Talmud** scholar and **halakhic** authority. Unlike Rashi's Bible commentary, which gives the meaning of each word and phrase, Nachmanides's is an explanation of broad themes. In the course of his work, he often disagrees with earlier commentators (including **Rashi**). He gives reasons for many of the commandments and, making use of the **Kabbalah**, shows how many events in the Bible are symbolic prophecies of the coming **messianic** age. He also wrote **responsa** and a clarification of difficult **halakhic** principles.

Nahum (*na-hum*) a prophet of the late 6th century BCE. His prophecy concerns Nineveh, a major Assyrian city which was conquered by the Babylonians in 612 BCE (compare **Jonah**), pointing out that any nation that oppresses Israel and fails to live justly must fall eventually.

Nahum, Book of the seventh book of **Trei Asar**, the Twelve Prophets. The book consists of three chapters. Chapter one stresses God's greatness and His power to save those who trust Him. The second chapter deals with the fall of Nineveh, the final chapter giving the reasons for its fall – pride, injustice and violence.

Nashim (*na-shim*) lit. women, the third section (called Order) of the **Mishnah**. Nashim deals with betrothal, marriage, divorce and vows.

Nazarenes Hebrew (*notz-rim*) name originally given to the Jewish followers of Jesus, who lived in Nazareth (Hebrew Natzeret). Whereas the English term refers specifically to that 1st century sect, the Hebrew notzrim still means Christians in general.

Nazi Party the National Socialist German Workers' Party that governed Germany from 1933–1945. The Party was formed in 1919 and launched vigorous propaganda aimed at appealing to the German people's need to rebuild its national pride after the defeat of World War I. Central to its political ideology was its struggle against the Jews. Nazi propaganda blamed Germany's defeat and her economic problems on the Jews and portrayed the Jewish people as an inferior race scheming to take control of the world. With this as its justification, the Nazi Party began restricting the rights of German Jews, expelling them and eventually herding them into concentration camps. Camps were established in most of the countries Germany conquered during World War II where the Jews were either used for slave labour or killed. ▶ See **final solution, Judenrein, Shoah**, map 4.

Nehemiah (*ne-hem-yah*) governor of Judah in the mid 5th century BCE. He rebuilt the wall of Jerusalem, making it secure against attack from hostile neighbours. By organising the entire population into a work force that toiled day and night, the wall was completed in 52 days. Troubled by the extreme poverty of some of the people, Nehemiah compelled the rich to give back property taken as security on loans. Together with Ezra, he re-established the **Torah** as the community's guide to life, making it possible for everyone to acquire a knowledge of it.

Nehemiah, Book of an account of Nehemiah's two terms of office as governor of Jerusalem, appointed by the Emperor of Persia. Chapters 1–13:3 deal with his first term, his rebuilding of the wall of Jerusalem, threats against him and his renewal of the covenant, which he conducted together with Ezra. The last part of chapter 13 deals with some of the problems of his second term.

Neilah (*ne-iee-lah*) lit. closing (the door), the concluding service for **Yom Kippur**, the Day of Atonement, so called because it comes at the end of the 40-day period of seeking forgiveness when, in a figurative

sense, the gates of heaven close. At the end of neilah a single note is blown on the **shofar** (ram's horn) to announce that the fast is over.

Neo-Orthodoxy new Orthodoxy – a movement that emerged in Germany during the latter half of the 19th century, associated mainly with Rabbi Samson Raphael **Hirsch**. It aimed at retaining Orthodoxy's commitment to traditional learning and observance of the commandments while, at the same time, adopting the ways of modern European (in particular German) culture. Unlike contemporary East European Orthodoxy, it accepted modern dress and shaving the beard, and provided education for women. ▶ See also **Hildesheimer, Jissroel-mensch**.

Ner Tamid (*ner ta-mid*) continual light, the light that never goes out, usually positioned above the **ark** in the synagogue. It symbolises the **menorah**, the seven branched oil lamp in the **Temple**, whose western

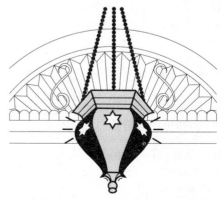

The **Ner Tamid** or continual light burns in every synagogue.

light (the light nearest to the **Holy of Holies**) burned continually. It is one of the ways in which Jews keep the memory of the Temple alive.

Nevelah (*ne-ve-lah*) an animal that died naturally, through disease or was killed without **shechitah**, the Jewish method of animal slaughter. If shechitah was not carried out properly, the animal is also nevelah. Jews are forbidden to eat nevelah since such animals may have died in pain.

Nevi'im (*ne-vi-im*) **1) Prophets 2)** the Books of the Prophets – **Joshua, Judges, Samuel, Kings, Isaiah, Jeremiah, Ezekiel, Hosea, Joel, Amos, Obadiah, Jonah, Micah, Nahum, Habakkuk, Zephaniah, Haggai, Zechariah** and **Malachi**. These books form the second part of the **Tenakh**, the Jewish Bible. They contain moral and religious teachings as well as important details of the earliest period of Jewish history. Jews regard these books as holy, but not as sacred as the **Torah**. ▶ See names of individual books for details.

New Year ▶ see **Rosh Hashanah**.

New Year for Trees ▶ see **Rosh Hashanah leilanot**.

Nezikin (*ne-zi-kin*) lit. damages, the fourth section (called Order) of the **Mishnah**. Nezikin deals with damages, compensation and fines, ownership, inheritance, business

contracts, the rules governing a court, examining witnesses and the punishments a court can impose.

Nidah (*ni-dah*) a woman from the moment she starts menstruating until after she has immersed herself in a **mikveh**. Although husband and wife live together, they are forbidden to have any physical contact during this time. It is sometimes compared to the engagement period when a couple express their love for one another in non-physical ways. ▶ See also **mikveh, taharat hamishpachah**.

Nine Days, The the period from 1st to 9th Av, the last nine days of the **Three Weeks**. This is a time of mourning for the loss of both Temples. In addition to the mourning customs observed during the Three Weeks, Jews neither eat meat nor drink wine (except on Sabbath, when no mourning is permitted).

Nisan (*ni-san*) the first month of the Jewish year, occurring in March–April; originally called Aviv, spring. Passover begins on 15th Nisan.

Nistarim (*nis-ta-rim*) hidden ones, learned, pious men who, during the 18th century, used to travel round the Jewish villages of Eastern Europe trying to encourage simple, unlearned Jews in their Jewish observance. They would conceal their scholarship (hence the name nistarim) and pretend to be simple labourers so that they could mix easily with the population. The nistarim were forerunners of the **Hasidic** movement. ▶ See **Baal Shem Tov**.

Nisuin (*Ni-su-in*) lit. uplifting, the final stage of marriage. Jewish marriage consists of two stages, **erusin**, where a couple are married but not yet living together and nisuin, when they set up home together. In ancient times there was often a year between the erusin and the nisuin. Today, the ceremonies are performed one after the other under the **huppah**, the marriage canopy.

Noachide Laws the seven laws communicated to Noah after the flood;

1) not to worship any being other than God

2) not to blaspheme

3) not to murder

4) not to steal,

5) not to commit acts of sexual perversion

6) not to eat the limb of a living animal (by extension, not to be cruel to animals)

7) to set up a system of justice. Jews regard these laws as binding on all humankind.

Numbers 4th book of the Bible, so called because it begins with a census of the Israelites (chapters 1–4); called **Bemidbar** in Hebrew.

Obadiah (*o-vad-yah*) a prophet whose dates are unclear; according to some authorities he is the Obadiah who hid the prophets from persecution in the time of **Elijah** (I Kings 18:13), according to others he lived after the **Babylonian exile**. The main theme of his prophecy is the destruction of Edom as a punishment for the way the Edomites treated Israel. According to the **Talmud**, Obadiah was himself an Edomite convert to Judaism.

Obadiah, Book of the 4th book of **Trei Asar**, the Twelve Prophets. It is the shortest book of the Bible, containing only 21 verses, mainly of prophecy against Edom. Verses 1–9 are similar in theme and language (though not in sequence) to **Jeremiah** 49: 7–22,

Old Testament a term used by Christians to refer to the **Tenakh**, the Jewish Bible, by which they distinguish it from their New Testament. Jews do not, as a rule, use the term since they have neither an Old nor New Testament; they simply have a 'Testament' ie the Tenakh. ► See also **Written Torah**.

Omer (*o-mer*) a measure of barley (about 40 cubic centimetres) cut on the 2nd day of **Passover** and offered in the **Temple**. ► See **sefirat haomer**.

Onen (*o-nen*) immediate mourners, plural onenim (*o-ne-nim*) . From the moment someone dies, close relatives become onenim. They are exempt from many of the commandments since they are occupied with the one overriding commandment of seeing that the body is prepared for burial. ► See also **avelut, chevra kaddisha**.

Orach Chaim (*o-rach cha-yim*) lit. the path of life, the first part of the **Arbaah Turim** and **Shulchan Aruch**, the major **codes** of Jewish law. Orach Chaim includes the **halachot** (laws) relating to everyday life such as prayer, blessings for food, Sabbath and festival observance.

Oral Torah the body of teachings,

starting with **Moses** and expanded upon by subsequent Jewish leaders, which was traditionally passed on by word of mouth. Towards the end of the second century CE, Rabbi **Judah the Prince** set many of these oral teachings down in writing to form the **Mishnah**.

Orthodox Greek *orthos doxa*, straight thinking; originally a term of derision used by the early **reformers** to refer to Jews who did not agree with the changes they were introducing into Judaism; now an accepted term for Jews who uphold Orthodoxy (► see next entry), though some Orthodox Jews find it meaningless and prefer not to use it.

Orthodoxy (► see previous entry) the belief that God gave the **Torah** at **Mount Sinai** and that all Jews are obliged to live by its teachings. This does not mean, as is sometimes thought, living by a rigid, unchanging system of laws but rather continually reapplying the Torah's teachings to ever changing conditions. Today, it has become common to speak of right-wing and centrist Orthodoxy; centrist Orthodox Jews being more willing to involve themselves with **secular** culture.

Out-marriage marrying outside of the Jewish community, ie a Jew marrying a non-Jewish partner; also known as intermarriage.

Pale of Settlement a strip of territory running from the Baltic Sea to the Black Sea, in which the Tsarist government allowed Jews to settle. Jews had not been permitted to live in Russia since the 15th century. When the Russians annexed part of Poland in 1722, they found themselves in possession of territory inhabited by thousands of Jews. In order to make sure that the Jews did not spread into Russia itself, they established the Pale as an area where Jews were allowed to live, although its exact extent varied under successive Tsars. Jews found outside the Pale without special permits were liable to be arrested and punished. The Pale was abolished after the Russian Revolution of 1917. ► See map 3.

Palestine a name for the **Holy Land** (► see **Israel 3**), derived from Pileshet, the Hebrew term for the land of the Philistines. It was also the name of a kingdom established by the crusaders in the Middle Ages. In 1922, Britain accepted the **Mandate** (ie administration) of Palestine from the League of Nations. Today, the name is used by those Arabs who still refuse to recognise the State of Israel. Jews use the term to refer to the same territory when speaking of the period before 1948, when Israel was established.

Parev or Parve Halakhah (*par-ev, par-ve*) Jewish law, forbids Jews to cook or eat meat and dairy foods together. Foods that are neither of meat or dairy origin, for example fruit, vegetables or soft drinks are called parev. Parev foods may be eaten with either meat or dairy dishes.

Passover ► see **Pesach**.

Pasul (*pa-sul*) unfit for sacred use, the opposite of kosher, eg a Torah scroll with a letter missing or a broken **lulav**, palm branch. ► See **kosher 2**).

Patriarchs Hebrew avot (*a-vot*) the fathers of the Jewish people, **Abraham**, **Isaac** and **Jacob**. They were unique in their time, about 38 centuries ago, in that they worshipped one God and served Him, not only with prayer and sacrifices, but also through acts of kindness and hospitality. ► See also **matriarchs**.

Pentateuch the Five Books of **Moses**; from the Greek, Pentateuchos, five-volumed. ► See **Torah**.

Pesach (*pe-sach*) Passover, a seven day festival (eight days outside Israel) that marks the Israelites' departure from Egyptian slavery about 3300 years ago. The first and last days are holy when no work may be done (other than food preparation), the middle days are **chol hamoed**, days when certain types of work are permitted. On Pesach, Jews do not eat bread or other grain products, apart from **matzah**. The main celebration centres on the **seder** meal at the beginning of the festival, when the events of the slavery and departure are retold. ▶ See **bedikat hametz, hametz, melechet avodah.**

Pesach sheni (*pe-sach she-ni*) lit. the second **Passover**; the 14th **Iyar**, one month after Passover, when people who were unable to offer the Passover sacrifice in the **Temple** because they were unclean or far away at the right time, had another opportunity to do so. There are no special observances for Pesach Sheni today, but some Jews make a point of eating **matzah**, unleavened bread, to keep the memory of it alive. ▶ See also **korban Pesach, shalosh regalim.**

Pharaoh a term the **Torah** uses for all the kings of Egypt. Several pharaohs were responsible for enslaving the Israelites, most notably Rameses II who reigned from 1290–1224 BCE and after whom a city (built by the Israelite slaves) was named (Exodus 1:11). The pharaoh who Moses negotiated with to gain the slaves' freedom was probably Merneptah (1224–1216 BCE).

Pharisees Hebrew perushim (*pe-ru-shim*) lit. separate ones; a Jewish sect that began to emerge in the mid 2nd century BCE and, by the 1st century CE had become the dominant group in Palestine, so called because they kept themselves separate from uncleanliness. The Pharisees regarded the Torah as the most important focus of Jewish life, as opposed to the **Sadducees** who upheld the importance of the **Temple**. In opposition to the **Zealots**, who put nationalism first, the Pharisees were able to reconcile themselves to living under Roman domination as long as they were permitted to continue teaching the Torah. They taught that the **Written Torah** could only be interpreted in terms of the **Oral Torah**. The Pharisees were the only one of the 1st century sects to survive the destruction of Jerusalem and the Temple in 70 CE, and their teachings formed the basis for the continuation of Judaism.

Pidyon haben (*pid-yon ha-ben*) redemption of the first-born son. Originally, first-born sons were intended to be priests. After the sin of the golden calf (Exodus 32:1–6), in which the first-born sons participated, this privilege was transferred to the tribe of Levi. To this day, first sons are born into a priestly role they cannot fulfil and so have a ceremony of redemption. Pidyon haben takes place when a baby is one month old.

Pikuach nefesh (*pi-ku-ach ne-fesh*) saving a life; in Jewish teaching all the commandments may be set aside to save a life, except the three cardinal sins – murder, idolatry and adultery.

Pilgrimage when the **Temple** stood, every Jew was expected to appear there three times a year, on **Pesach, Shavuot** and **Sukkot** with offerings. After the Temple was destroyed, pilgrimage as a religious duty ceased to exist in Judaism. Today, some Jews regard it as a personal pilgrimage to visit the holy sites such as the **Hakotel Hamaaravi**, the last remaining wall of the Temple or the tomb of the **Patriarchs** in Hebron.

Pinsker, Leon (1821–1891) prominent member and eventual head of **Hibat Zion**. For much of his life, Pinsker believed that the Jews of Russia should assimilate into the surrounding culture. His views began to change after the **pogroms** of 1871. The second wave of pogroms in 1881 convinced him that there was no future for Jews in Russia and he began advocating emigration to a new homeland. In 1882, Pinsker set down his views in his book, **Autoemancipation**. At the Kattowitz conference in 1884, Pinsker was elected to head a project to encourage Jews to take up agriculture and to support those

who had settled in **Palestine**. Together with Rabbi Shemuel **Mohilever** and Max **Lilienblum**, he worked to achieve this. After 1891, when the Turkish government clamped down on Jewish immigration, Pinsker sought to save Jews from persecution by resettling them in Argentina.

Pirkei Avot (*pir-key a-vot*) lit. Chapters of the Fathers, often called Ethics of the Fathers, a volume of **Mishnah** that deals entirely with Jewish ethics. Pirkei Avot is a collection of sayings of major rabbis (mainly) of the first two centuries CE, though some of its teachings go back at least two centuries earlier. Its main concern is the value of **Torah** study and guidance in character development. In the synagogue, a chapter of Pirkei Avot is studied each **Sabbath** afternoon between **Pesach**, Passover, and **Rosh Hashanah**, the New Year.

Pogrom Russian (*pog-rom*) destruction and bloodshed; a term that refers to the attacks on the Jews of Russia between 1881–1884, again from 1903–1906 and once more during the years 1917–1921. The pogroms began in Elizavetgrad in April 1881 and eventually spread to 160 Jewish towns and villages throughout the **Pale of Settlement**. The pogroms were one of the main reasons for Jews leaving Eastern Europe in the two decades before 1914 (when World War I began and all travel stopped) and migrating to Britain, America, South Africa,

Australia and other countries. ▶ See map 3.

Posek (*po-sek*) **1)** as a noun, one who decides matters of **halakhah**, Jewish law, plural poskim (*pos-kim*). Although, in practice, any **rabbi** can decide questions of halakhah, the term posek is usually reserved for rabbis of international repute whose decisions are regarded as having great authority. **2)** as a verb, to decide matters of halakhah.

Priest ▶ see **cohen**.

Promised land the **Holy Land**, roughly the same as modern Israel; God promised each of the **Patriarchs**, the fathers of the Jewish people, that it would one day belong to their descendants (Genesis 12:7, 26:3, 28:13).

Prophets men and women with whom God communicated. Although the **Torah** describes God speaking to the **patriarchs** and others, the main period of Jewish prophecy extended from **Moses** to just after the rebuilding of the second **Temple**. Jews regard Moses as the greatest of the prophets, God's communication to him being more direct than to anyone else. Following Moses, the early prophets (from **Joshua** to **Samuel**) were mainly military leaders; the middle prophets (**Elijah** and **Elisha**) were miracle workers. The later prophets (from **Amos** on) were largely, teachers of morality. There were also entire communities of prophets whose words were never written down for posterity, as well as false prophets. Jews believe that God sent prophets to other nations too.

Prophets, Books of ▶ see **Neviim**.

Prosbul (*pros-bol*) a Greek word meaning a document in which a creditor signs debts over to the **bet din**, as rabbinic court, who are empowered to collect them even after **shemittah**, the year in which debts are cancelled. Prosbul was introduced by **Hillel** in the 1st century BCE, who saw that, as the shemittah year approached, people became reluctant to lend money, knowing that the loan might be cancelled. Prosbol made it possible for poor people to obtain loans.

Protocols of the Elders of Zion a document concocted by the Russian secret police in about 1905, supposed to contain Jewish plans for taking over the world. The Tsarist government used it as justification for passing anti-Jewish laws, and it has been quoted by **anti-semites** ever since.

Proverbs, Book of Hebrew Mishlei (*mish-ley*) the 2nd book of the **Ketuvim**, the Holy Writings, a guidebook for righteous living set out in the form of short sayings. The themes covered include the value of acquiring wisdom, warnings against associating with the wicked, the consequences of sin (in particular adultery and idolatry) and against greed. It concludes with a description of the ideal woman. According to the **Talmud**, the book was written by King **Solomon**.

Psalms, Book of Hebrew Tehillim (*te-hi-lim*) a collection of 150 prayers and praises of God. It is the 1st book of the **Ketuvim**, the Holy Writings. According to the **Talmud**, the psalms were written by King **David**, who incorporated prayers written by ten other people, including **Moses**. Some psalms refer to particular incidents in David's life (eg, Psalm 34 is a prayer of thanksgiving he said when he escaped from a Philistine king); some were written to be used in the **Temple** which David knew his son would build. Today, psalms are used extensively in Jewish worship, with some reserved for special occasions (eg **Hallel**).

Purim (*pu-rim*) Akkadian for dice, a celebration held on 15th **Adar** to mark the overthrow of **Haman**, a Grand Vizier of King Ahasuerus, who, in the 5th century BCE, planned to kill all the Jews in the Persian Empire. The plot was thwarted by **Esther**, a Jewish queen of Ahasuerus, at whose request the Jews were granted permission to defend themselves. The day is called Purim after the dice Haman threw to determine which day would best suit his gods for a massacre. Jews celebrate Purim by sending each other gifts of food and giving money to the poor. They also read the **Book of Esther**.

Pushke Yiddish (*push-ke*) a charity collection box.

Qumran (*kum-ran*) the ruins of a settlement near the Dead Sea. It was inhabited between about 150 BCE – 70 CE by people who are presumed to have written the **Dead Sea Scrolls**. The people at Qumran lived a monk-like existence, they never married and spent their days in prayer, meditation and working for the community. They called themselves 'the sons of light', referring to other Jews as the 'sons of darkness'. They believed that God would one day send an army of angels to drive out the Romans as well as all sinful Jews, after which they would become God's chosen ones. Most scholars believe that they were a branch of the **Essene** sect.

Rabbi 'my master', a term of respect similar to the English 'sir'. Originally, the term referred to teachers of the **Torah** (other than prophets) who had received **semichah**, authorisation to decide matters of **halakhah** (Jewish law). Today, most rabbis act as communal leaders and do not issue halakhic rulings. Many still fulfil a teaching role in some form.

Rachel (*ra-chel*) second wife of **Jacob** and mother of **Joseph** and Benjamin; one of the matriarchs, the mothers of the Jewish people. Rachel died giving birth to Benjamin. Her tomb in Bethlehem is Judaism's third most holy site.

Rambam ▶ see **Maimonides**

Ramban ▶ see **Nachmanides**

Rashi (*ra-shi*) Rabbi Shelomoh Yitzchaki (1040–1105) foremost Bible and **Talmud** commentator. Rashi wrote commentaries on almost all the books of the **Tenakh** and Talmud, though some were completed by his students. In his Bible commentary, he sets out to give the plain meaning of the text, though he makes considerable use of **midrash**. He also explains the grammatical structure of unusual

words, though his system of grammar is sometimes difficult to follow since it differs from the system used today. His Talmud commentary is a phrase by phrase explanation of the Talmudic discussions, often anticipating the very question a student is likely to ask. Rashi was also highly esteemed as an **halakhic** authority and wrote **responsa**.

Rav another form of rabbi.

Rebbe (*re-be*) variation of rabbi, leader of a hasidic group; learned and pious men who care for the spiritual (and often physical) wellbeing of their **hasidim**, followers; plural rebbeim (*re-bei-im*). Hasidim turn to their rebbe for advice and blessings on a wide variety of matters. The degree of their authority varies among different hasidic communities.

Rebekah Hebrew Rivkah (*riv-kah*) wife of **Isaac** and his cousin, second of the **matriarchs**, the mothers of the Jewish people. According to tradition, she was selected for her role because, in spite of growing up among evil people, she resisted following in their ways. When Abraham's servant was sent to find a wife for Isaac, he stood at a well and prayed for someone who, if he asked her for a drink, would offer to water his camels as well. Rebekah came by and made the required offer (Genesis 24:12–27).

Reform Movement during the late 18th century, **haskalah**, the movement for integrating Jews into the wider society, had brought about widespread assimilation, particularly in Germany. By the early 19th century, **secularised** Jews had begun introducing reforms into the synagogue. They shortened the service, prayed in German and began singing to organ accompaniment – in effect, modelling their Judaism on the Lutheran Church. During the 1840s, leaders of the reforming congregations held a number of conferences, aiming to consolidate the trend into an organised movement. In this same period, there was a division into a radical wing, whose spokesmen called for far reaching changes such as abolishing **circumcision** and discontinuing the use of **Hebrew** as the language of prayer, and a moderate wing that wanted small scale changes. The radical strand became very influential in American Reform and the British **Liberal Movement**; British Reform was always less extreme. Nevertheless, even the British Reform Movement has redefined **halakhah**, Jewish law, to make it possible to work on the **Sabbath** day, no longer observes **taharat hamishpachah**, disregards **mamzerut** and annuls marriages where obtaining a **get**, a Jewish divorce, proves difficult. ► See also **Frankel, Geiger, Hirsch, Holdheim, Montefiore.**

Reines, Rabbi Yitchak Yaakov (1839–1915) one of the founders of religious Zionism. Although educated in some of the leading **yeshivot**, Talmudic academies of the day, he believed that Jews should receive a **secular** education alongside their Talmudic studies. His attempt to establish an institution where this would be put into practice was vigorously opposed by other rabbis (compare **Hildesheimer**). As an active supporter of **Hibat Zion**, he worked with Rabbi Shemuel **Mohilever** to develop settlements in **Palestine** where work would be combined with **Torah** study. Rabbi Reines was a personal friend of Theodor **Herzl** and worked ceaselessly to encourage east European rabbis to support **Zionism**. He became the first head of the **Mizrahi** Movement.

Responsa Hebrew sheelot uteshuvot (*she-e-lot u-te-shu-vot*), questions and answers; letters sent by individuals or communities to renowned **halakhic** experts, asking for their opinions or rulings. Responsa began during the 6th century, when Jewish communities were widely scattered and it was no longer possible to have immediate access to the major religious authorities who were, at that time, in **Babylon**. With the passage of time, responsa became a standard way of clarifying difficult halakhic issues or elucidating a passage of **Talmud** or **Tenakh**. Today, responsa deal with halakhic issues arising from modern technological or medical advances.

Rosh Chodesh (*rosh cho-desh*) the beginning of a new Jewish month, occurring when the moon appears to have grown so small that it cannot be seen from earth. Since the moon orbits the earth every month ($29\frac{1}{2}$ days), Rosh Chodesh is sometimes celebrated over two days. In the synagogue, part **Hallel** is said, followed by a Torah reading describing the Rosh Chodesh service in the Temple and **musaf**, an additional service. Psalm 104 is also read, praising God for maintaining the order of nature.

Rosh Chodesh groups formed by women in recent years to use Rosh Chodesh as a time for strengthening their Jewish commitment. Rosh Chodesh was chosen since, traditionally, it was a time when women did not do any work. (This is still partly observed in some communities.) In these groups, women have revived some ancient Rosh Chodesh customs to make their meetings distinctly womens' events. Activities vary from one group to another, though most include giving **tzedakah**, charity.

Rosh Hashanah (*rosh ha-sha-nah*) the Jewish New Year, 1st and 2nd Tishrei; the only festival observed over two days in Israel as

well as the rest of the world. Jews believe that, on Rosh Hashanah, God decides the fate of all His creatures and they pledge themselves anew to keep God's commandments. The **shofar**, ram's horn, is blown on both days (unless the first day is a Sabbath).

Rosh Hashanah leilanot (*rosh ha-sha-nah le-i-la-not*) lit. New Year for Trees, 15th **Shevat**. When the Temple stood it was the cut off date for tithing fruit; anything tithed prior to that date belonged to the previous year's crop, fruit tithed after it was part of the new crop. Today, the custom has developed of eating fruit on that day as a means of keeping the memory of it alive. In Israel there are tree planting ceremonies, especially for schools.

Ruach hakodesh (*ru-ach ha-ko-desh*) lit. the holy spirit, a form of divine communication lower than prophecy. Those who possess ruach hakodesh do not hear God's voice as the **prophets** did, but their thoughts and feelings will be guided. They may not always be aware that they have it.

Ruth (*root*) a Moabite woman who joined the Jewish people, the great grandmother of King **David**. Ruth married into an Israelite family that had fled to Moab to escape a famine. There, she had developed a love for Judaism. When her husband and father-in-law died, her aged mother-in-law decided to return to her home in Bethlehem. Ruth insisted on going with her. At first, the two women were shunned and suffered poverty. However, Ruth gradually gained a reputation for modesty and compassion, resulting in them both being accepted by the people of Bethlehem. According to tradition, Ruth was blessed with living to an extremely old age.

Ruth, Book of one of the **Chamesh Megillot**, the Five Scrolls. According to the **Talmud**, the book was written by **Samuel**. It is read in the synagogue on **Shavuot**.

S

Saadia Gaon (882–942) the father of Jewish philosophy. In Saadia's day, **Babylon** was still a major centre of Jewish life. However, the community was dividing rapidly into a number of sects, each with a slightly different understanding of Judaism. The most important deviant sect (and the most dangerous) was the **Karaite Sect**, which rejected the entire **Oral Torah** and insisted that Jews should be guided by scripture alone. Many Jews were also confused as a result of religious disputations with Muslims. Saadia's book, *Beliefs and Opinions* (written in Arabic so that the people could understand it) argued against these sects so successfully that, a century after his death, Karaite thinkers were still trying to refute his ideas. Saadia demanded an intelligent approach to Judaism, insisting that people should try to understand the commandments. In **halakhah**, although Saadia did not compile a **code**, he was the first to set down his rulings in logical sections. He also did pioneering work in Hebrew grammar, his first publication being a rhyming dictionary which he wrote at the age of 20.

Sabbath ► see **Shabbat**.

Sadducees Hebrew Tzedukim (*tze-du-kim*), a sect of 1st century Judeans whose membership included many priests. The name derives from their founder, Zadok. They rejected the authority of the **Oral Torah**, and did not believe that there would be a resurrection of the dead. ► See also **Essenes, Pharisees, Zealots**.

Samuel Hebrew Shemuel (*she-mu-el*) the last of the **Judges**. Samuel's mother dedicated him to the service of God at an early age when she took him to live with Eli, the High Priest. A wise and holy man, he was Israel's undisputed spiritual leader during the late 10th century BCE. In his latter years, Samuel anointed **Saul** king over Israel, though he himself had mixed feelings about a monarchy. When Saul did not wipe out the Amalekites as Samuel commanded him, he anointed the young **David** as king in Saul's place.

Samuel, Book of takes the history of Israel from the birth of **Samuel** almost to the death of **David**. According to the **Talmud**, the book was written by Samuel himself except for the chapters dealing with events after his death, which were added by two prophets, Nathan and Gad. Due to the book's length, later scholars divided it into two parts known as I and II Samuel.

Sanctuary ▶ see **mishkan**.

Sandak (*sun-dak*) the person who holds a baby boy during his circumcision. It is a great honour to act as sandak. The child's grandfather or some other older and respected person is usually invited.

Sanhedrin (*san-hed-rin*) **1)** the supreme Jewish court (▶ see **bet din hagadol**); **2)** a council of rabbis convened by Napoleon in 1807 because he wanted it to issue rulings making it possible for Jews to integrate into French society.

Sarah Hebrew Sarah (*Sa-rah*) wife of **Abraham**, the first Jew, and first of the **matriarchs**, the mothers of the Jewish people. After God promised Abraham and Sarah children, she remained childless as a test of their faith. At the age of 90, by a miracle, she gave birth to **Isaac**. According to Jewish tradition she worked, together with her husband, to spread knowledge of God among the moon worshipping people of Ur.

Sarah imenu (*sa-rah i-me-nu*) 'our mother **Sarah**', a term of reverence and endearment Jews use, recognising Sarah as their first mother.

Saul (*sha-ul*) Israel's first king. During the 10th century BCE, many Israelites felt that only a king could unite the tribes sufficiently to free them from Philistine oppression (▶ see **Judges**). Saul was chosen for his piety and his imposing physical appearance. After some initial success, Saul found his reputation becoming eclipsed by that of his son-in-law, **David** and made several attempts to kill him. He believed that David was a threat to his own son, Jonathan (David's closest friend), becoming king after him. At the battle of Mount Gilboa, the Philistines inflicted a crushing defeat on Israel, and Saul and Jonathan were killed.

Scheneirer, Sarah (1883–1935) pioneer of Jewish women's education and founder of the **Bet Yaakov** movement. Sarah Scheneirer had little formal education but so loved immersing herself in Jewish books that, as a child, people called her the 'little pious one'. While earning her living as a dressmaker, she came under the influence of the **Neo-Orthodox** movement in Germany, in particular Rabbi Samson Raphael **Hirsch**. Appalled by the growing religious laxity of Polish women, she decided to take action. In 1918 she opened a school in her dressmaker's shop in Cracow with 25 girls aged between 15 and 18, calling it **Bet Yaakov** – the House of Jacob. Subsequently, she received support from **Agudat Yisrael**, whose leaders appreciated the need to educate young women and, in 1926, a second school was opened. By the time Sarah Scheneirer died, nine years later, **Bet Yaakov** schools were catering for 80,000 students right across eastern and central Europe. ▶ See also **Kahan**.

Schneerson, Rabbi Menachem Mendel (1902–1994) leader of **Habad Hasidim** for 44 years, Jewish thinker and communal planner. Rabbi Schneerson was known for sending his followers to set up Jewish educational programmes all over the world, and for initiating campaigns to make Jews aware of the commandments. Rabbi Schneerson also encouraged Jews to contribute to the moral advancement of humanity at large. He wrote extensively and his published talks fill many volumes. A year after his death, the US government awarded him the Congressional Medal of Honour, bearing the inscription *letaken haolam*, 'for bettering the world'.

Science of Judaism ▶ see **Wissenschaft des Judenthums**.

Secular Jews Jews who, by and large, do not regard religion as important and generally keep very little or nothing at all of the religion. However, being Jewish does not depend on what people believe or practise since anyone who is born of a Jewish mother or has converted to Judaism is a Jew. For this reason, secular Jews are fully Jewish. ▶ See next entry

Secularism the belief that one can live one's life without religion. Secularism began with the Enlightenment, a movement that arose during the early 18th century and attacked, among other things, the authority of the Church. Later that century, the **Haskalah** movement introduced secularism into Jewish life. ▶ See previous entry.

Seder (*se-der*, usually rhymes with raider) lit. order **1)** one of the six divisions of the **Mishnah**. **2)** The Passover meal, so called because the meal follows a set sequence of stages during which the Israelites' slavery in Egypt and their departure by God's intervention are discussed. On the table are various symbolic foods representing, in different ways, slavery and freedom.

Seder plate a plate used at the seder, the Passover meal, with spaces sunken into its surface to act as containers for the items of food necessary for conducting the seder.

▶ See **betzah, carpas, haroset, maror, zeroa.**

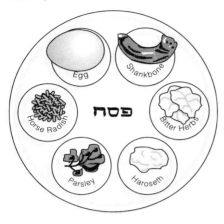

A **seder** plate.

Sefer Torah (*se-fer to-rah*) scroll of
the Torah, the Five Books of **Moses**,
plural sifrei Torah (*sif-rei to-rah*).
Each scroll is handwritten by a
sofer, a trained scribe, who writes in
columns on sheets of parchment
made from animal skins, which
must be obtained from a **kosher**
animal. Writing a sefer Torah takes
about a thousand working hours.
Torah scrolls are the Jews' most
sacred objects and are kept in the
synagogue **ark** when not in use.
When they are carried to the **bimah**,
the reading desk, for public reading,
the entire congregation rises as a
mark of respect for God, whose
words are on the scroll.

Sefirat haomer (*se-fi-rat ha-o-mer*) lit. the counting of the omer, the
period of 49 days between **Pesach**,
Passover, and **Shavuot**, the Feast of
Weeks; so called because it begins on
the day the **Omer**, the offering of the
barley harvest, used to be brought to
the **Temple**. During sefirat haomer,
Jews count the days and weeks until
Shavuot, which completes the
celebration of Pesach.

Selichot (*se-li-chot*) prayers for
forgiveness (from the Hebrew
selach, pardon). **Sephardim** rise
early throughout the month of **Ellul**
to say selichot in preparation for
Rosh Hashanah, the New Year.
Ashkenazim begin selichot during
the latter part of the month. ▶ See
also **teshuvah, yom hadin.**

Semichah (*se-mi-chah*) lit. leaning,
rabbinical authorisation, ie authority
to decide on matters of **halakhah**,
Jewish law; originally it involved an
older rabbi laying his hands on the
head of the newly qualified student.
Today, people obtain semichah by
studying **Talmud** and halakhah
(Jewish law) and taking an
examination, often oral. Successful
students are awarded a te'udat
semichah, a certificate of rabbinic
authorisation. It is sometimes
referred to as rabbinical ordination.
This is not correct. Ordination means
being admitted to holy orders, it is
appropriate to Christian priests but
not to rabbis.

Seminary institution of advanced
Jewish learning for girls; the
equivalent of the **yeshivah**.
Seminary studies include Bible,
Jewish law, literature and history,
midrash, prayer and the **Hebrew**
language. Some seminaries offer

vocational training too. Most girls who go to a seminary do so solely to improve their Jewish knowledge (compare **yeshivah**). Many seminary graduates become teachers. ▶ See also **Scheneirer**.

Sephardim (*se-far-dim*) originally the Jews of Spain and Portugal, now a term for oriental Jews in general (as distinct from **Ashkenazim**). The Spanish and Portuguese Jews began migrating following persecutions at the end of the 14th century. In 1492, all Jews who refused to become Christians were expelled from Spain. Some stayed (▶ see **Marranos**) but about a quarter of a million fled to North Africa, Italy and Turkey; many migrated further east to Egypt, Syria and Iraq. Others went north to Holland and, from there, to England and America. Many Sephardim, particularly those around the Mediterranean coast, used **Ladino** as a common language. Those further east spoke **Hebrew** and Arabic.

Sevivon (*se-vi-von*) spinning top; ▶ see **dreidle**.

Shabbat (*sha-bat*) the Sabbath, the 7th day of the Jewish week, the period from sunset on Friday until nightfall on Saturday. Shabbat is not a 'day of rest' in the plain sense but a holy day. It is a time of rest from physical toil (Deuteronomy 5:14), indeed, Jews are forbidden to do many kinds of work (▶ see **melachah**), but the purpose of this is to leave people free to follow

spiritual pursuits. On Shabbat, Jews spend more time at prayer and **Torah** study than during the rest of the week. The Torah commands Jews to observe Shabbat as a reminder that God created heaven and earth and then 'rested' (Exodus 12:11). Jews like to celebrate Shabbat with their families, singing songs at the table and telling stories about the great men and women of the Jewish past.

Shabbat hagadol (*sha-bat ha-ga-dol*) lit. the great Sabbath, the Sabbath before Passover, so called because of the miracle that occurred on that day when, according to Jewish tradition, the first-born sons of Egypt, knowing that they were to be killed in a plague, rose up in rebellion against **Pharaoh**. ▶ See also **eser makot**.

Shabbat mevarchim (*sha-bat me-va-re-chim*) lit. Sabbath of blessing, the Sabbath before **Rosh Chodesh**, a new Jewish month, when the time of the coming month is announced and the congregation pray that it should be a month of receiving God's blessings.

Shabbat shalom (*sha-bat sha-lom*) lit. a Sabbath of peace, a greeting and parting used by Jews on the Sabbath.

Shabbat shuvah (*sha-bat shu-vah*) the Sabbath that occurs during the **Aseret Yemei Teshuvah**, the Ten Days of Returning (ie before **Yom Kippur**, the Day of Atonement). It is called after the opening words of the **haftarah**, the prophetic reading for that day, Shuvah Yisrael, 'Return Israel' (Hosea 14:2).

Shabbos (*sha-bos*) **Ashkenazi** pronunciation of **Shabbat**, the Sabbath.

Shabbetai Zevi (1626–1676) a false messiah who became the focus of an international movement. Learned in both **Talmud** and **Kabbalah**, many in his home town of Smyrna considered him insane because of his odd behaviour (eg having himself married to a **Torah scroll** and celebrating **Pesach, Shavuot** and **Sukkot** in the same week). In 1665, he visited the **Holy Land** where a local visionary declared him to be the long awaited redeemer. The whole population of Gaza accepted him, followed by other communities too. The movement spread through Europe where Jews began fasting and repenting to prepare to meet the messiah, although many prominent rabbis distanced themselves from it. Shabbetai was arrested by the Turkish authorities as he was leading thousands of his followers to the **Holy Land**, and imprisoned. He was given the choice of accepting Islam or death. He chose Islam. After his conversion, in which he was joined by his wife and closest followers, the messianic movement collapsed. However, a handful of his followers were so convinced that they continued to believe in him.

Shacharit (*sha-cha-rit*) the morning service. Shacharit consists of six parts; early morning blessings, in which Jews thank God for supplying all their needs, selected readings from the **Psalms**, the **Shema** and its accompanying blessings, the **Shemoneh Esrei**, said silently while standing, a prayer for forgiveness (which, in some versions of the prayer, includes confession) and Aleinu, the concluding prayer. On Mondays and Thursdays, Sabbaths, **Rosh Chodesh** (beginning of new month), festivals and fasts, shacharit includes a public Torah reading. It is said during the early part of the morning, at the time when the daily morning sacrifice used to be offered in the **Temple**. ► See also **Abraham**.

Sheliach tzibbur (*she-li-ach tzi-bur*) lit. one appointed by the congregation, ie the person who leads the prayers in the synagogue. For Jews, the ideal way to pray is together with the community. This makes it necessary for someone to lead and set the pace, rather like the conductor of an orchestra, so that people go through the service together. Whoever is selected as sheliach tzibbur (it does not have to be a rabbi) must be familiar with the services for various occasions. ► See also **chazan**.

Shalom (*sha-lom*) peace; a Jewish greeting and parting.

Shalosh regalim (*sha-losh re-ga-lim*) lit. three occasions ie **Pesach**,

Shavuot and **Sukkot**, the three occasions in the year when all Jews were expected to make a pilgrimage to the Temple bearing offerings. They are sometimes called the three foot festivals – a common error due to confusing the Hebrew 'regel' occasion, with an identical word meaning foot.

Shamash (*sha-mash*) lit. servant.
1) a person who sees that the synagogue is kept in order, that people have prayer books and that the Torah scrolls are checked regularly. ▶ See also **gabbai**;
2) a candle used to light the **Hanukah** lights; the shamash or 'servant candle' stands apart from the other lights either by being placed higher or adjacent to the row of lights.

Shatnez (*sha-at-nez*) the presence of wool and linen in the same garment. Jews are forbidden to wear this (Deuteronomy 22:11). The Torah gives no reason for this; it is one of the **chukim** (commandments) that are observed as acts of faith, ie trusting that God commanded them for a purpose even though humans cannot fathom what that purpose is. Also spelt shaatnez.

Shavua tov (*sha-vu-a tov*) a good week, Jewish greeting and parting used on Saturday nights when, at the end of the Sabbath, the new week begins.

Shavuot (*sha-vu-ot*) a festival that commemorates the giving of the **Torah** on **Mount Sinai**. It occurs on 6th **Sivan** (and 7th as well outside Israel). Although there are festive services in the synagogue, Shavuot has no special rituals like other festivals. However, various customs have grown up over the years such as decorating the synagogue with flowers, eating dairy foods, reading the **Book of Ruth** and staying up the entire first night to study the Torah or say **Tikun**, a digest of several classical Jewish texts. ▶ See also **sefirat haomer**.

Shechinah (*she-chi-nah*) lit. resting or dwelling, the presence of God, ie the place where God's presence rests. Shechinah is a confusing term – if God is everywhere, it is not possible to refer to a particular place as the place where His presence rests. However, the real meaning is not where God is but where His presence can be felt. The Shechinah can, therefore, be anywhere, although Jews believe that some places are particularly conducive to feeling God's presence, ie the site of the **Temple**. Also spelt Shekhinah.

Shechitah (*she-chi-tah*) 'slaughter': the Jewish method of killing animals for food (and, when the **Temple** stood, for sacrifice). The animal's throat is cut with a razor-sharp knife, slicing through the carotid arteries, the blood vessels that carry blood to the brain When these arteries are severed, blood pressure in the brain plunges to zero, causing immediate loss of consciousness and death. Shechitah is one of the most painless methods of animal slaughter. ▶ See also **chalaf, kosher, nevelah, shochet.**

Shekel (*she-kel*) lit. weight, the standard silver coin in ancient Israel, so called because silver was originally weighed when making a purchase (eg Genesis 23:16). Some first century coins bear the inscription shekel shakul, 'a shekel by weight'. Today, the shekel chadash, new shekel, is the currency of modern Israel.

Sheloshim (*she-lo-shim*) lit. thirty, the first month after a funeral. After **shivah**, the first week of mourning (which is included in the sheloshim), mourners start resuming their normal lives. However, they neither cut their hair and nails nor listen to music. ▶ See also **avelut, onen.**

Shema (*she-ma*) lit. hear, a declaration of basic Jewish beliefs said twice a day at the morning and evening services, called after the opening words, Shema Yisrael, 'Hear Israel'. The declaration consists of three paragraphs; **Deuteronomy** 6: 4–9, declaring the oneness of God, Deuteronomy 11: 13–21, a statement of the **covenant** relationship between God and the Jewish people, and **Numbers** 15: 37–41, an acknowledgement that God took the Israelites out of Egypt.

Shemini Atzeret (*she-mi-ni a-tze-ret*) the gathering of the eighth day, ie the eighth day after the beginning of **Sukkot**. It marks the completion of the annual cycle of Torah readings and the beginning of the next cycle. Outside Israel, Shemini Atzeret extends over two days, the second day being called **Simchat Torah.**

Shemittah (*she-mit-ta*) lit. release, the seventh year when no agricultural work is to be done on the soil of Israel, other than that which is needed to prevent the land from deteriorating. At the end of the shemittah year, all debts between Jews are cancelled except where a **prosbul**, a document handing over debts to the court, has been written.

Shemoneh esrei (*she-me-neh es-rei*) lit. the eighteen, a silent prayer in which Jews ask God for their needs, originally it contained 18 blessings, although a 19th was added during the 1st century CE. The first three blessings and the last three are always the same; the middle blessings differ on weekdays, Sabbaths and festivals. Also called **amidah**, the standing prayer. It is said in each of the three daily services, and is the main part of **musaf**, the additional service for Sabbaths, Rosh Chodesh (new month) and festivals.

Shemot (*she-mot*) the second book of the **Tenakh**, the Jewish Bible; called **Exodus** in English. Shemot continues where **Bereshit, Genesis,** leaves off, with the story of how the Egyptians enslaved the Israelites, the ancestors of the Jews. It tells of how

God sent Moses to lead them out of slavery, how they crossed the Red Sea and received the **Torah** at **Mount Sinai**. It concludes with the details of the **mishkan**, the portable Temple the Israelites built in the desert.

Sheva berachot (*she-va be-ra-chot*) the seven blessings that form the final part of a marriage ceremony (▶ see **bircat nisuin**). In communities that observe sheva berachot, marriage celebrations continue for a full week, with a festive meal each evening in a different place. At the end of each meal, the seven blessings are recited. Through usage, the term sheva berachot is often taken to refer to the meal itself. ▶ See **erusin, nisuin**.

Shevarim (*she-va-rim*) a note blown on the **shofar**, ram's horn, consisting of three short blasts . ▶ See **tekiah, teruah**.

Shevat (*she-vat*) 11th month of the Jewish year, corresponding roughly with January–February. 15th Shevat is the **New Year for Trees**.

Shir Hashirim (*shir ha-shir-im*) ▶ see **Song of Songs**.

Shivah (*shi-vah*), lit. seven, the week of intense mourning following a funeral. During shivah, bereaved relatives stay together where possible. They sit on low chairs with a tear in their clothes and do not cut their hair or nails. Men do not shave. All the mirrors in the house will be covered so that no-one should pay attention to their appearance. A candle will be kept burning symbolising the departed soul. The mourners stay at home where services will be held three times each day and they will say **kaddish yatom**, the declaration of God's praise. Throughout the week, friends and relatives will spend time with the mourners and offer them words of comfort. ▶ See also **avelut, onen, sheloshim**.

Shmuesen (*shmu-sen*) Yiddish lit. talks, a term used in the **yeshivot**, Talmudic academies, for the ethical talks delivered by the teachers. These talks usually complement the individual ethical guidance given to students . ▶ See **musar**.

Shoah (*sho-ah*) see map 4; the systematic destruction of European Jewry by the Nazis. From the time the **Nazi Party** came to power in Germany in 1933 to the outbreak of World War II in 1939, they carried out a massive propaganda campaign to portray the Jews as the ultimate enemies of civilisation – they were said to be corrupting the German people, controlling the banks and universities and plotting to take over the world. Throughout this period, the Nazis gradually restricted the German Jews' citizen rights and, from 1937 on, began sending them to concentration camps. The purpose of all this was to change the way the German people thought about their Jews and to prepare them to accept the extermination of the Jews as a necessity. In 1941, when Germany invaded Russia, the campaign of extermination began. The Germans set up concentration camps in all the countries under their control. There, Jews who were old, sick or otherwise unfit for work were sent to the gas chambers. Those who could work were forced into slave labour. When they could no longer work, they too were gassed. Others died from the savage beatings, the forced marches or the typhus and dysentery that ran through the camps unchecked. By the end of the war in 1945, six million Jews had perished – one and a half million of them children. ▶ See map 4.

Shochet (*sho-chet*) person who slaughters animals for consumption by Jews, plural shochetim. Shochetim usually specialise either in the slaughter of cattle or poultry.

Shofar (*sho-far*) a bugle like instrument made by hollowing out the horn of any **kosher** animal such

The sound of the **shofar** represents the cry of the soul yearning to be reunited with God.

as sheep, goat or gazelle (but not cows), though rams' horns are normally used. It is blown at the end of morning prayers during the month of **Ellul** (except on Sabbath and the last day of the month) to remind worshippers that **Rosh Hashanah**, the New Year, is approaching. Most importantly, it is blown during the additional service of Rosh Hashanah (except when Rosh Hashanah occurs on a Sabbath).

Shteibel (*shtee-bel*) Yiddish little room, plural shteiblach. Originally, shteiblach were small rooms in people's houses set aside for prayer. Eventually, the word came to mean small synagogue. Today shteiblach are mainly associated with the **hasidic movement**.

Shul (*shool*) Yiddish term for a **synagogue**, used by **Ashkenazi** Jews.

Shulchan Aruch (*shul-chan a-ruch*) lit. prepared table, a **code of halakhah**, Jewish law, compiled by Rabbi Yosef Caro and published by him in 1565. It followed the four part division of the **Arbaah Turim**, an earlier code. Unlike that work, which included numerous rabbinic opinions, the Shulchan Aruch normally gave only the accepted halakhot, rulings, and presented them in short, concise paragraphs. It became so influential that all subsequent digests of Jewish law have been based on it.

Shushan Purim (*shu-shan purim*) the day after **Purim**, celebrated as Purim in cities that had walls at the time of **Joshua**, such as **Jerusalem**. So called because Shushan, the capital of the Persian Empire, was where the main action of the Purim story took place. ▶ See also **Esther**.

Sidra (*sid-rah*) a portion of the **Torah** read on Sabbath mornings; plural sidrot (*sid-rot*). There are 54 sidrot; the longest contains 176 verses, the shortest has only 30. By reading a sidra each week, Jews complete the whole Torah in the course of a year. On some Sabbaths, two sidrot are read.

Siddur (*si-dur*) prayer book, so called because the prayers are set out in a **seder**, order; plural siddurim (*si-du-rim*). Although Jews pray mainly in **Hebrew**, most siddurim printed today give translations into English or other modern languages. Many also offer worshippers directions for following the services and some have notes explaining the prayers as well as readings for private meditation. There are also children's siddurim with illustrations and simplified translations or summaries of the prayers.

Simchat Torah (*sim-chat to-rah*) the Rejoicing of the Torah, celebrated on 23rd Tishrei, except in Israel where it occurs on 22nd – the same day as **Shemini Atzeret**. On Simchat Torah, Jews complete the annual cycle of Torah readings by reading the final **sidra**, portion, of **Devarim**, Deuteronomy. They then commence the new cycle by reading the creation story at the very beginning of **Bereshit**, Genesis. Simchat Torah is a joyous occasion and is celebrated by dancing round the synagogue with the Torah scrolls and distributing sweets to children.

Sivan (*si-van*) the third month of the Jewish year, occurring around May–June. The festival of **Shavuot** takes place on the 6th (and, outside Israel on the 7th as well) of Sivan.

Sofer (*so-fer*) a scribe, plural soferim (*so-fe-rim*); one who writes and corrects **Torah scrolls** as well as **mezuzot** and the small scrolls inside **tefillin**. A sofer must also be available to write a **get**, document of divorce, at any time and sometimes ketubot, **marriage** documents too.

Sofer, Rabbi Moses (1762-1839) Rabbi of Pressburg, Hungary and one of the foremost **halakhic** authorities of his day. He established a **yeshivah**, Talmudic academy, in Pressburg, from where he led the struggle against **Reform** by encouraging Torah education and using his influence to establish his most talented students in rabbinic positions far and wide. He opposed **haskalah**, the movement for **secularising** Jewish life and kept apart from the struggle for **emancipation**. He believed that the traditional Jewish way of life was morally and spiritually superior to that being offered by the new secularising movements and fought to preserve it.

Solomon Hebrew Shelomoh (*she-lo-moh*), reigned c. 960-920 BCE, son of **David** and Bathsheba; third king of Israel. Solomon's reign was a time of peace and prosperity, marred only by the royal building projects that were carried out with forced labour. Solomon himself was renowned for his wisdom and the lavish splendour of his court. His greatest achievement was the building of the first **Temple**, a project that took seven years. The **mishkan**, the portable temple built by **Moses** in the desert, was dismantled and stored away and Solomon invited all Israel to a 14 day celebration.

Song of songs Hebrew Shir Hashirim (*shir ha-shi-rim*) one of the Chamesh Megillot, the five scrolls. It takes the form of a love song, describing, often in striking poetic imagery, a country girl's love for a shepherd and her encounter with the king. Jews have always taken it to be an allegory, referring to the love of God and the Jewish people for one another. **Rabbi Akiva** declared, 'If all the books of the Bible are holy, Song. of Songs is holy of holies'. It is read in the synagogue on **Passover**. Some Jews read it every Friday afternoon before the **Sabbath**.

Sukkah (*su-kah*) lit. booth or hut, plural sukkot (*su-kot*), a temporary dwelling with a covering of leaves used by Jews during the festival of **Sukkot** (▶ see next entry). The sukkah calls to mind the dwellings the Israelites made for themselves in the desert after they left Egypt. Throughout the week of the festival, Jews eat their meals and entertain their friends in the sukkah rather than in the house. Some sleep there too. Traditionally, Jews decorate their sukkot by hanging fruit from the leafy covering.

A **sukkah** used during **Sukkot**.

Sukkot (*su-kot*) an eight day festival (seven in Israel) which marks the Israelites' trek through the desert on their way to their **promised land** (called **Tabernacles** in English). Throughout the festival, Jews live in temporary, leaf-covered dwellings (▶ see previous entry). During the festival prayers, they hold their **arbaat haminim**, four plant species, and move them from all six directions towards their hearts, symbolising the flow of God's blessings. ▶ See also **hakafot, Hoshanah Rabbah**.

Synagogue Greek for place of gathering. ▶ See **bet haknesset, bet hamidrash**.

Taanit Bechorim (*ta-a-nit be-cho-rim*) the fast of the first-born sons. It takes place on 14th Nisan, the day before Passover and is a token of thanksgiving to God for sparing the first-born sons of the Israelites when those of the Egyptians were killed. ▶ See **eser makot**.

Taanit Esther (*ta-a-nit es-ther*) the fast of Esther, observed on 13th Adar, the day before **Purim**. It marks the anxious months when the Jews of the Persian Empire (in effect, all the Jews in the world) were under threat of annihilation. People start celebrating Purim while still fasting to recreate the feeling of the turnover 'from sorrow to gladness, from mourning to festivity' (Esther 9:22). ▶ See also **Esther, Haman**.

Tabernacles ▶ see **Sukkot**.

Taharah (*ta-ha-rah*) usually translated purity or cleanliness. These are misleading translations since taharah is a spiritual state; **1)** a condition of spiritual preparedness for which there is no term in English. The opposite of taharah is **tumah**, a state of spiritual unpreparedness; **2)** the process of preparing a dead body for burial. As part of the procedure, the **Chevra Kaddisha**, burial society, wash and

sometimes immerse the body in a **mikveh**, immersion pool.

Taharat hamishpachah (*ta-ha-rat ha-mish-pa-chah*) family purity; the set of laws governing marital relationships. Married couples cease physical contact from the moment the wife starts menstruating (Leviticus 18:19). When her period stops, she waits a further week – known as 'the seven clean days', ie days without menstrual flow – and then visits the **mikveh**, a special pool where she immerses herself in water. Upon her return, husband and wife may resume their sexual relationship. ▶ See also **nidah, tevillah**.

Tahorot (*ta-ho-rot*) lit. purities, the sixth section (called Order) of the **Mishnah**. Tahorot deals with the ways in which ritual impurity is passed to people, utensils and foods, and the means by which they may become pure.

Tallit (*ta-lit*) a four cornered garment with **tzizit**, fringes attached to each corner, plural tallitot. ▶ See next two entries.

Tallit gadol (*ta-lit ga-dol*) lit. large cloak, a rectangle of wool or silk cloth worn by Jewish males during morning prayer; usually called tallit for short. The tallit gadol is worn across the back and draped over the shoulders with the corners left hanging in front and behind, so that the wearer is surrounded by the fringes. In some communities, married men wear it over their heads like a cowl. During the last few generations, many men have taken to wearing tiny tallitot that they drape around their necks like scarves, giving rise to the mistaken idea that the tallit is a 'prayer shawl'. In fact, prayer cloak or robe would be more correct. After death, the tallit is wrapped round the body as a shroud.

A man wearing a **tallit gadol** for morning prayer.

Tallit katan (*ta-lit ka-tan*) small cloak, a smaller version of the tallit gadol (▶ see previous entry) that Jewish males wear throughout the day. It has a central hole for the head and drapes over the body front and back. People often wear them under their shirts. In some communities,

boys are given their first tallit katan on their third birthday.

A **tallit katan** is worn during the day.

Talmud (*tal-mud*) a commentary on the **Mishnah**, also called **gemara**. The term usually refers to the Babylonian Talmud and, less frequently to the slightly older Jerusalem Talmud (▶ see next entry). Each Talmud takes the form of recorded discussions about the Mishnah and also contains teachings, parables and stories stretching over many centuries.

Talmud Bavli the Babylonian Talmud, a collection of rabbinic discussions about the **Mishnah** that took place in the academies of **Babylon** (now Iraq) between 200 – 500 CE. It was compiled by Rav Ina and Rav Ashi. Written in Eastern **Aramaic**, the Talmud Bavli became the basis upon which all subsequent **halakhah**, Jewish law, is based. It is still the main subject of study in **yeshivot**, Talmudic academies.

Talmud Yerushalmi the Jerusalem Talmud (sometimes called the Palestinian Talmud), a commentary on the **Mishnah** similar to the Talmud Bavli but considerably shorter and compiled a century earlier. It is written in Western **Aramaic** and is a record of discussions that took place in the academies of Judea (Israel). It is not as widely studied as the Bavli.

Talmud Torah (*tal-mud to-rah*) **1)** study of the Torah; **2)** with the **Ashkenazi** pronunciation (*tal-mud to-rah*) a system for providing Jewish education for pupils attending non-Jewish schools. Talmud Torah classes are usually held on synagogue premises after school hours and on Sunday mornings. Pupils learn **Hebrew** as well as the **Torah**, prayers and Jewish history. Also called **cheder**.

Tammuz (*ta-muz*) fourth month of the Jewish year. The 17th is a fast that marks the beginning of 'the Three Weeks', a period of sadness. ▶ See **shivah asar b'Tammuz.**

Tanna (*ta-na*) plural tannaim, the rabbis whose teachings are included in the **Mishnah** and **Tosefta**. They were active mainly during the 1st and 2nd centuries CE. Their teachings, interpreted and expanded by the **amoraim**, the rabbis who followed, and incorporated into the two **Talmuds**, have been considered authoritative by subsequent generations of Jews.

Targum translation of the **Torah** or **Tenakh** into **Aramaic**; plural targumim (*tar-gu-mim*). The need for targumim arose during the 1st and 2nd centuries CE, when most Jews were using Hebrew. Most widely used is the Torah targum of Onkelos, a Roman who converted to Judaism in the 2nd century CE. The targumim are not only translations, they sometimes explain the text.

Tashlich (*tash-lich*) lit. throwing away, a prayer said on the first day of **Rosh Hashanah**, the New Year, when Jews ask God to remove their sins. It is said on the banks of a river to symbolise the verse, 'and You will cast all their sins into the depths of the sea' (Micah 7:19). If the first day of Rosh Hashanah is a Sabbath, tashlich is said on the second day.

Tefillah (*te-fi-lah*) **1)** prayer, the word may refer to a particular prayer or to prayer in general; **2)** one of the **tefillin**, the leather boxes tied to the head and upper arm that Jewish adult males wear during morning prayer. ▶ See next two entries.

Tefillah shel rosh (*te-fi-lah shel rosh*) a leather box bound to the head with a strap. It has four compartments, in each of which is a small handwritten scroll containing the first two paragraphs of the **shema** (Deuteronomy 6:4–9 and 11:13–21) as well as Exodus 13:1–10 and 13: 11-16. It is worn in the centre of the forehead just above the hair line, in accordance with

Deuteronomy 6:8. The tefillah shel rosh reminds the wearer that he must serve God with his mind, ie develop thoughts of justice and compassion towards people and love for God.

A man wearing a **tefillah shel rosh**.

Tefillah shel yad (*te-fi-lah shel yad*) a leather box bound to the upper arm with a strap. It has one compartment containing a single scroll upon which are written the same four passages as in the tefillah shel rosh (see previous entry). It is bound to the biceps muscle of the left arm inclining slightly towards the heart, the strap then being wound round the arm and hand. A left-handed person wears it on the right, as it must always be on the weaker arm. It reminds the wearer that he must serve God with his heart, ie develop feelings of justice and compassion towards people and love for God.

Tefillin (*te-fi-lin*) plural of tefillah (▶ see previous two entries). The tefillin are made from the hide of **kosher** animals, as is the parchment of the scrolls they contain.

Tehillim (*te-hi-lim*) ▶ see **Psalms**.

Tekanah (*te-ka-nah*) a ruling enacted by a **Bet Din**, rabbinical court, for the benefit of the community or by a synagogue committee for the benefit of the congregation, plural tekanot (*te-ka-not*). Most tekanot are only intended to apply to Jews in a particular locality. Those enacted by the rabbis in **Talmudic** times apply universally. ▶ See also **tikun haolam**.

Tekiah (*te-ki-ah*) a single long sound blown on the **shofar**, the ram's horn, together with shorter notes known as **shevarim** and **teruah**, throughout the month of **Ellul** but mainly on **Rosh Hashanah** (the New Year). The shofar blowing on Rosh Hashanah ends with a tekiah gedolah – an exceptionally long note.

Temple ▶ see **bet hamikdash**.

Ten Commandments Hebrew (*a-se-ret ha-dib-rot*) lit. ten statements, usually known as the Ten Commandments (although they actually contain more than ten). They are:
- Know that I am the Lord your God who brought you out of slavery in Egypt
- You must not have any other gods besides Me
- You must not use God's name without good reason
- Remember to keep the Sabbath as a holy day; do not do any work
- Respect your father and your mother

- You must not murder
- You must not steal
- You must not commit adultery
- You must not give false evidence
- You must not desire someone else's house, wife or anything that belongs to another person.

The Torah describes how the Israelites heard these commandments at **Mount Sinai** (Exodus 20:1–14).

Tenakh (*te-nakh*) the Jewish Bible. Tenakh is not a real word, but made up from the initial letters of the words **Torah** (the Five Books of Moses), **Neviim** (the books of the Prophets) and **Ketuvim** (the holy writings). The three letters make TNK, pronounced Tenakh or Tanakh. The Tenakh is also known as the **Written Torah** to distinguish it from the **Oral Torah**, the traditions handed down by word of mouth.

Teruah (*te-ru-ah*) very short note blown on the **shofar**, the ram's horn (▶ see **tekiah**). A teruah consists of at least nine notes blown in a quick, clipped way.

Teshuvah (*te-shu-vah*) lit. returning, used to mean repentance. The term reflects the Jewish attitude to repentance, seeing it not so much as turning away from sin but rather of returning to God. In Jewish thinking, people are always connected with God. Sin can place a barrier between the person and God, but can never break the connection. In these terms, turning to God is simply coming back to one's real self, ie returning.

Tevet (*te-vet*) the tenth month of the Jewish year, roughly corresponding to December–January. The 10th is a fast commemorating the start of the Babylonian siege of Jerusalem in 587 BCE that resulted in the destruction of the first **Temple**.

Tevillah (*te-vi-lah*) immersion. A week after a married woman's period has stopped, she immerses herself in a **mikveh**, a special immersion pool. Before her tevillah she bathes, having first removed all jewellery and make up, since nothing may come between her skin and the water of the mikveh. A female attendant watches to ensure that she immerses totally. After tevillah, she and her husband may resume sexual relations. ▶ See also **nidah, taharat hamishpachah**.

Tevillat kelim (*te-vi-lat ke-lim*) immersion of utensils. Newly bought crockery, cutlery and cooking utensils not manufactured by a Jew are immersed in a mikveh, a pool of natural water, before being used for the first time. This is an act of purification and reflects the sanctity in everyday things that Judaism demands. Only metal, glass or glazed kitchenware require immersion.

Three Weeks, The the period from 17th **Tammuz** to 9th **Av**. These were the weeks of fighting in the streets of Jerusalem that ended in the first **Temple** being destroyed by the Babylonians in 586 BCE, and the second Temple by the Romans in

70 CE. Jews observe these three weeks as a period of mourning when they neither cut their hair nor listen to music. ▶ See also **avelut, shivah asar b'Tammuz, tishah b'Av.**

Tikun (*ti-kun*) lit. correction, a digest of several Jewish holy books, containing extracts from the **Tenakh, Mishnah, Zohar** and other works, that some Jews read throughout the night of **Shavuot**. The name derives from the tradition that, before they received the **Torah** at Mount Sinai, the Israelites made the mistake of going to sleep. By staying up all night to read tikun, Jews 'correct' their ancestors' mistake.

Tikun haolam (*ti-kun ha-o-lam*) lit. correcting (or repairing) the world, a term used for rules made by rabbis to prevent abuses. For example, the **Talmud** mentions the problems that could have arisen when a man sent a **get**, a document of divorce, to his wife who was in a different town and then, changing his mind, annulled it in his local court. The wife, knowing nothing of this and believing that she was divorced, might remarry only to discover later that she had been committing adultery. To prevent this happening, the rabbis ruled that husbands should not be permitted to do this, as a matter of tikun haolam.

Tishah b'Av (*ti-sh ah-b'av*) the 9th day of the month of **Av**. A fast held to mourn for the two **Temples**, both of which were destroyed on that day – the first in 586 BCE and the second in 70 CE, as well as many other

tragedies. It is the second most important fast after **Yom Kippur**, the Day of Atonement. On Tishah b'Av, morning prayers are said without **tallit** or **tefillin**, these being worn in the afternoon. The Book of **Lamentations** is read, as well as **kinot**, dirges.

Tishri (*tish-ri*) 7th month of the Jewish year, roughly corresponding to September–October. Tishri is virtually filled with holy days; the first two days are **Rosh Hashanah**, the New Year; the 3rd is a fast, **Tzom Gedaliah**, the 10th is **Yom Kippur**, the Day of Atonement, the week of **Succot** starts on the 15th, the 22nd (and 23rd too outside Israel) is **Shemini Atzeret** and **Simchat Torah**.

Torah (*to-rah*) lit. instruction. **1)** the first five books of the **Tenakh**, the Jewish Bible. Jews regard these as the holiest part of the Tenakh; **2)** the whole Tenakh, ie the **Written Torah**, **3)** the whole of Jewish teaching, ie the Written and **Oral Torah** collectively. ▶ See also **Ketuvim, Neviim, sefer Torah.**

Torah im derech eretz (*to-rah im de-rech e-retz*) lit. **Torah** study with 'the way of the land', a term in **Pirkei Avot**, the volume of **Mishnah** dealing with ethics, that originally meant Torah study coupled with an occupation. Rabbi Samson Raphael **Hirsch** used it to mean commitment to the Torah's teachings together with an appreciation of general culture. It became his slogan and summed up his notion of the ideal Jew. ▶ See also **Jissroel-mensch.**

Torah scroll ▶ see **sefer Torah**.

Tosafot (*to-sa-fot*) lit. additions, a collection of commentaries on the **Talmud** written in France and Germany between the 12th–14th centuries. The tosafot usually analyse specific points rather than explain the text systematically. They are found along the outside margins in modern printed editions of the Talmud.

Tosefta (*to-sef-ta*) **Aramaic** additions, a collection of **halakhic** rulings not included by Rabbi **Judah the Prince** in his **Mishnah** but arranged according to the Mishnah's order. It is usually found at the back of modern editions of the **Talmud**.

Trefah (*trey-fah*) lit. torn, a term used for food that Jews are forbidden to eat; the opposite of **kosher**. The origin of the term is the prohibition of eating meat from animals that had been torn (ie injured) and unable to live out their natural life span.

Trei Asar lit. the twelve, a collection of fairly short prophetic books spanning several centuries. Trei Asar contains **Hosea, Joel, Amos, Obadiah, Jonah, Micah, Nahum, Habakkuk, Zephaniah, Haggai, Zechariah**, and **Malachi**. ▶ See individual entries for details.

Trumpeldor, Joseph (1880–1920) Jewish soldier who distinguished himself fighting with the Russians in the Russo–Japanese war, in spite of being wounded and having his left arm amputated. He believed that Jews should establish collective settlements in **Palestine** and form an army to defend themselves. In 1912, he went to Palestine and worked on a **kibbutz**, helping to organise the defence of Jewish settlements in the region. During World War I, he formed the Zion Mule Corps and worked with **Jabotinsky** to form a Jewish legion and liberate Palestine from Turkish rule. Later, he went back to Russia and helped set up a **Zionist** youth movement that trained young Jews for life in Palestine. He returned to Palestine in 1919 and began reorganising the defence of Jewish settlements in Upper Galilee. In March 1920, he was mortally wounded defending Tel Hai against an Arab attack.

Tumah (*tu-mah*) usually translated impurity or uncleanliness. This is not correct since tumah is a spiritual state for which there is no exact term in English. ▶ See also **taharah**.

Twelve tribes during the first few centuries following **Joshua's** conquest of the **Holy Land**, the Israelites lived within tribal borders. The twelve tribes are Reuben, Simeon, Levi, Judah, Issachar, Zevulun, Gad, Asher, Dan, Naftali, Menasseh, Ephraim and Benjamen, each one descended from one of **Jacob's** sons. Menasseh and Ephraim were descended from **Joseph**, who did not have a tribe named after him. The tribe of **Levi** had no territory of its own, the Levites being scattered among the other tribes. ▶ See map 1.

Tzaar baalei chaim (*tza-ar ba-a-lei cha-yim*) lit. pain (or suffering) of a living creature. Jews are absolutely forbidden to cause unnecessary tzaar baalei chaim. They also see this prohibition as applying to all humankind and, therefore, one of the requirements of a civilised life. ▶ See **Noahide Laws.**

Tzedakah (*tze-da-kah*) lit. righteousness, helping those in need by giving of one's money or possessions. Tzedakah is often translated charity, though this is not entirely accurate since 'charity' implies doing a good deed. In Jewish terms, giving tzedakah is something that is expected rather than a voluntary 'good deed'. ▶ See also **gemilut hassadim.**

Tzizit (*tzi-tzit*) fringes worn on the corners of the **tallit gadol** and **tallit katan**, four cornered garments worn by Jewish males at morning prayer and throughout the day respectively. Four threads, usually of wool, are doubled over to make eight fringes; they are worn in compliance with Numbers 15:38–39. Originally, one of the threads was dyed blue, but knowledge of how to make the blue dye has been lost. Today all tzizit are white.

Tzom Gedaliah the fast of Gedaliah, a fast that marks the assassination of Gedaliah ben Ahikam, governor of **Jerusalem** after the destruction of the first **Temple**. Gedaliah had worked carefully for two years to rebuild good relations with the Babylonian authorities and regain their confidence. He was murdered at the **Rosh Hashanah**, New Year feast, by a Jewish prince jealous of his success. The remaining Jews in Jerusalem fled to Egypt and all hope of restoring the Temple was lost. Since fasting is not permitted on Rosh Hashanah, Tzom Gedaliah is observed on the following day, the 3rd **Tishri.**

U

Ultra orthodox a term meaning those who, in the popular mind, are thought of as the most strict in their religious observance. It generally refers to (mainly **hasidic**) Jews who wear 19th century east European dress and speak **Yiddish.** In this sense it is a meaningless term since the distinguishing feature of such Jews is that they wish to have as little contact as possible with **secular** culture rather than that they are more observant than other Jews.

Vayikra (*va-yik-ra*) the third book of the **Tenakh**, the Jewish Bible; called Leviticus in English. Vayikra gives many details of the sacrifices that were offered in the **mishkan**, the portable Temple the Israelites built in the desert. It lists the food Jews may and may not eat and lays down the laws for observing festivals.

Vidui (*vi-dui*) confession, a short confession is included in some versions of the daily prayers (▶ see **shacharit**) and occupies an especially prominent place in the prayers for **Yom Kippur**, the Day of Atonement. However, neither rabbis nor priests hear confession; Jews only confess to God, never to a person.

Wissenschaft des Judentums German, Science of Judaism, a movement that emerged in Germany during the early 19th century. Its exponents, many of whom were connected with the early **Reform** movement, aimed to apply the analytical study methods current in the universities to the laws, prayers, literature and history of Judaism. At first, the academic world did not take Wissenschaft seriously and its leaders established their own institutions of learning. These were the forerunners of Jewish Studies departments in modern universities.

Written Torah the **Tenakh**, the Jewish Bible, as distinct from the **Oral Torah**, the traditions handed by word of mouth. The Written Torah began with **Moses** and continued through the writings of the prophets till **Malachi** in the 5th century BCE who brought the Written Torah to a close.

Yad (*yud*) lit. hand. A pointer used during Torah readings to show the place to the person called to recite the blessings (▶ see **aliyah 2**); so called because it is usually made in the form of a rod ending in a hand with an extended index finger pointing. The reader uses a yad to point to the text rather than his own finger since the **Torah scrolls** are sacred and Jews try to avoid touching them unnecessarily.

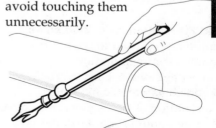

A **yad** is used during Torah readings.

Yad Vashem (*yad va-shem*) lit. a monument and memorial (see Isaiah 56:5), the Holocaust memorial in Jerusalem, established just after World War II. It contains photographs, artefacts and documents relating to the Holocaust, some of which are exhibited publicly. It also contains eye-witness accounts supplied by camp survivors and those who fought in the **ghetto** uprisings or as partisans. The Hall of Names records the names of the victims and, in the Memorial Hall, an eternal flame burns amid the names of concentration camps placed around the floor in Hebrew and English. On **Yom Hashoah**, Holocaust Memorial Day, special services are held there. Many Jews visit Yad Vashem as a personal **pilgrimage**. ▶ See map 4.

Yamim noraim (*ya-mim no-ra-yim*) lit. days of awe, ie **Rosh Hashanah**, the Jewish New Year, and **Yom Kippur**, the Day of Atonement; so called because Jews believe that during those days God judges His creatures and decides their lot for the coming year.

Yarmulke (*yar-mul-ke*) Yiddish, ▶ see **kippah**.

Yarzheit (*yar-tzite*) **Yiddish** for anniversary, used to refer to the annual commemoration of someone's death. On a yarzheit, **kaddish yatom**, the mourners' declaration of God's glory, is said. A candle, symbolising the departed soul, burns for 24 hours. In some communities a small celebration is held to mark the soul's annual ascent through the heavenly spheres. ▶ See also **avelut**.

Yemenites the origin of the Jewish community of Yemen (Southern Arabia) is thought to go back to the first century BCE. The Yemenite Jews are, therefore, neither **Sephardim** nor **Ashkenazim**. The spread of Islam to Yemen meant that the Jews lost most of their rights and were frequently persecuted. Yemenite Jews began migrating to Palestine in the late 19th century. Both Yemenite Jews and Muslims saw the establishment of the State of Israel in 1948 as the hand of God and, in 1949, the remaining Jews left for Israel in what has come to be known as 'Operation Magic Carpet'.

Yeshivah (*ye-shi-vah*) lit. [place of] sitting, a **Talmudic** academy, plural yeshivot (*ye-shi-vot*) . The yeshivah is the oldest form of Jewish college. The main topic studied is the **Talmud Bavli**, Babylonian Talmud, though some time is given to **Tenakh**, Bible and **halakhah**, Jewish law. Most yeshivot have no set course of study – students continue studying the Talmud, gaining proficiency and moving up into higher classes as they do so. There are regular lectures and boys prepare for them and revise them by working in pairs (▶ see **chavruta**). The most able students do not attend any class, but study together in pairs, only consulting the lecturers when they need to clarify some point. The majority of boys who attend yeshivah do not go there to become rabbis but attend simply to advance their own knowledge of Judaism. The girls' equivalent is called a **seminary**.

Yichud (*yi-chud*) lit. togetherness, the final stage of the wedding ceremony when bride and groom spend a short while alone together as a statement that they are now husband and wife. They usually use the opportunity to break their fast. ▶ See also **huppah**.

Yiddish (*yi-dish*) a language similar to German, once spoken by Jews right across Eastern Europe. Jewish books and newspapers were printed in Yiddish and there were even Yiddish theatres. Today, it is the main spoken language in **Hasidic** communities; other **Orthodox** Jews use it too, though not as their main tongue. It is also the language of instruction in many **yeshivot**, Talmudic academies. Dialects vary and it is possible to identify Jews' countries of origin by their pronunciation of Yiddish as well as the local words they incorporate into their usage (compare **Ladino**). ▶ See map 3.

Yochanan ben Zakkai, Rabbi a disciple of **Hillel** and the foremost Jewish leader in the period following the Roman destruction of Jerusalem and the **Temple** in 70 CE. Shortly before Jerusalem fell, Rabbi Yochanan had himself smuggled out of the city. Appearing before Titus,

the Roman commander, he gained permission to set up a council of rabbis at Yavneh. There, he brought together a number of rabbis who guided the Jewish community through the religious and political crisis of the destruction. By planning the direction Judaism would take in the post-destruction era, they ensured its survival.

Yom Haatzmaut (*yom ha-atz-ma-ut*) Israel Independence Day, the anniversary of 14 May 1948, when **David Ben Gurion** declared the State of Israel. Yom Haatzmaut is celebrated on its date according to the Jewish calendar, 5th **Iyar** (although sometimes it is celebrated on the 4th).

Yom Hadin (*yom ha-din*) lit. Day of Judgement, a name for **Rosh Hashanah**, the Jewish New Year; so called because, in Jewish belief, this is the day God weighs up the deeds of all people and decides their situation for the coming year.

Yom Hashoah (*yom ha-sho-ah*) Holocaust Remembrance Day, 27th **Nisan**. In synagogues throughout the world, prayers are said on behalf of the six million Jews who perished between 1933 and 1945 at the hands of the **Nazis**. ▶ See also **Shoah, Yad Vashem** and map 4.

Yom Hazikaron (*yom ha-zi-ka-ron*) lit . Day of Remembrance, another name for **Rosh Hashanah**, the Jewish New Year; so called because, in Jewish belief, that is the day when God calls to mind the deeds of all human beings.

Yom Kippur (*yom ki-pur*) the Day of Atonement, an annual 25 hour fast when Jews pray for forgiveness for their sins. It is the holiest day in the Jewish year; Jews believe that the decisions God makes on **Rosh Hashanah**, New Year, concerning each person, are sealed on Yom Kippur.

Yom tov lit. a good day, a term Jews use to refer to the festivals, the equivalent of the Hebrew **chag**; 'gut yom tov' being a common **Yiddish** greeting and parting used on a festival (compare Gut Shabbos). It is often mispronounced as 'Yontof'.

Yom Yerushalayim (*yom ye-ru-sha-la-yim*) Jerusalem Day. East **Jerusalem** came into Jordanian

hands in 1948; a barbed wire fence divided the city into Jewish and Arab sectors. For 19 years, Jews were not permitted to visit their holiest site, the last remaining wall of the Temple (▶ see **Hakotel Hamaaravi**). In 1967, Israel regained control of the whole of Jerusalem and it became one city again with total freedom of access to all holy sites, Jewish, Christian and Muslim. Yom Yerushalayim is celebrated on 28th **Iyar** in the Jewish calendar.

Yoreh Deah (*yo-reh de-ah*) lit. teaching knowledge, the second part of the **Arbaah Turim** and **Shulchan Aruch**, the major **codes** of Jewish law. Yoreh Deah includes laws relating to kosher food, mourning customs, circumcision, and oaths as well as the special agricultural laws that apply in Israel (eg tithes).

Z

Zealots Jews who opposed the Romans prior to and during the war of 66–70 CE. There were several Zealot groups, each under its own commander. Although they were extremely courageous men, the various groups were so fiercely independent that they preferred to fight the Romans separately rather than work together. Even after the Roman armies had surrounded

Jerusalem, they still squabbled and fought among themselves. By the time they saw the seriousness of their situation and began to co-operate, it was too late for effective resistance. ▶ See also **Massada**.

Zechariah a prophet of the late 5th century BCE and a contemporary of **Haggai**. Zechariah urged the Jews who had recently returned from

Babylonian exile to rebuild the **Temple**. However, while stressing the importance of the Temple and its observances, Zechariah also stressed the need for moral virtue. Many of his prophecies take the form of visions with symbolic meaning, sometimes in the presence of an angel who explains them.

Zechariah, Book of the 11th book of **Trei Asar**, the Twelve Prophets. The first eight chapters describe visions seen by **Zechariah**, in which an angel explains their meaning. Most of the visions relate to the Jews who had recently returned from **Babylonian exile**. Chapters 9–14 are prophecies, often of destruction.

Zephaniah Hebrew (*tze-fa-ne-yah*) prophet of the mid 7th century BCE and contemporary of **Jeremiah**. Zephaniah supported King Josiah (to whom he was related) in overthrowing the idolatrous cults that King Menasseh had encouraged. He taught that years of idolatry, lax morals and heathen ways had aroused God's anger and that the only hope lay in repentance, for which God was giving them one final chance. He believed that the coming judgement would not destroy the nation entirely but that (as **Isaiah** had taught years earlier) a remnant would survive, purified and ready to do God's will.

Zephaniah, Book of the 9th book of **Trei Asar**, the Twelve Prophets. It falls into five sections;

(i) chapters 1:2–18, prophecy of God's coming judgement, (ii) chapters 2:1–15, prophecies against Judah's neighbours, in particular old enemies such as Ammon and Moab, (iii) chapters 3:1–7, denouncing the sinful people of Judah, especially the leaders, (iv) chapters 3:8–13, a reference to the period after God's judgement when all nations will know Him, (v) chapters 3:14–20, the people of Judah will again rejoice in God's blessings.

Zeraim (*ze-ra-im*) lit. seeds, the first section (called Order) of the **Mishnah**. Zeraim begins with a volume on prayer and then deals with agricultural matters such as crops that must be assigned to the poor, tithing farm produce and the **shemittah** year when the soil lies fallow.

Zeroa (*ze-ro-a*) lit. arm; a shank bone, usually burnt , placed on the **seder plate** to call to mind the korban **Pesach**, the Passover lamb Jews would offer and eat when the **Temple** stood.

Zeved habat (*ze-ved ha-but*) lit. the gift of a daughter, a naming ceremony for baby girls practised in some **Sephardi** communities. Any time between a week and a month after a daughter is born, her parents bring her to the synagogue, usually on a Sunday so that relatives and friends can be there. Her parents give the child her name and the rabbi blesses her. The ceremony is followed by a small celebration.

Zion (*tzi-yon*) lit. foremost, prominent; the name given to Jerusalem after King **David** made it his capital. Later, the name came to refer to the Holy Land as a whole. It was used in this sense by members of the **Hibat Zion** and the **Zionist** movements.

Zionism essentially Zionism is the belief that the Land of Israel is the homeland of the Jewish People. Jews have held this belief for over 3000 years. In that sense, the belief is much older than the term Zionism, which was not in use before the late 19th century. At that time, Zionism referred to the political movement founded by Theodor **Herzl**, that campaigned for a Jewish state in **Palestine**. Since 1948 when the State of **Israel** was established, Zionism has become concerned with supporting the Jewish state by fundraising, encouraging people to settle there and defending Israel's interests in the political and commercial arenas.

Zionist 1) as a noun, one who supports Zionism (▶ see above); **2)** as an adjective, relating to Zionism.

Zionist Congress a body formed by Theodor **Herzl** to bring **Zionists** and **Hovovei Zion** together so that they could discuss issues relevant to their cause and decide on policy. The first congress was held in Basle in 1897; its success was summed up by Herzl who wrote, 'At Basle I founded the Jewish State'. Subsequent congresses were held at various European locations (the fourth congress took place in London in 1900). Since the 23rd congress (1951) all congresses have been held in Jerusalem.

Zohar (*zo-har*) the Book of Splendour, the main work of **Kabbalah**, Jewish mysticism. Written in **Aramaic**, much of it takes the form of a commentary on the **Torah**, giving the inner, mystical meaning of the verses. It also contains stories about the 1st century sage, Rabbi Shimon ben Yohai who, in Jewish tradition, is the father of mysticism and whose teachings make up most of the *Zohar*. It was first published in the late 14th century by a Spanish mystic, Moses ben Shem Tov of Leon.

Zunz, Leopold (1794–1886) one of the founders of Wis**senschaft des Judenthums** (Science of Judaism). While at university, Zunz had absorbed scientific study methods and wanted to set up a similar system for studying Judaism, in particular Jewish history. In 1819, Zunz co-founded the 'Society for the culture and science of Judaism' and began editing a journal to which Jewish intellectuals were invited to contribute articles. His overriding aim was to have the study of Judaism recognised as an academic subject in the universities but, in 1884, his proposals were rejected by the Prussian minister of culture. Zunz rejected traditional Jewish learning and was dismissive of the **Talmud** and **Kabbalah**. Instead, he tried to show that Jewish literature and culture were part of the intellectual life of humanity.

Map 1: Tribal territories in ancient Israel

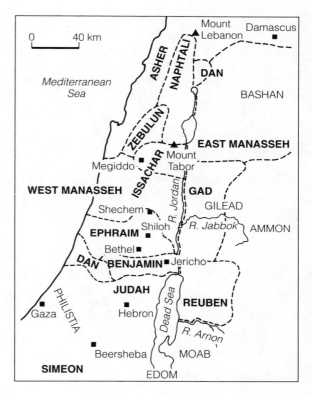

Map 2: Israel and Judah in the 8th century BCE

Map 3: The Pale of Settlement

Map 4: The Holocaust

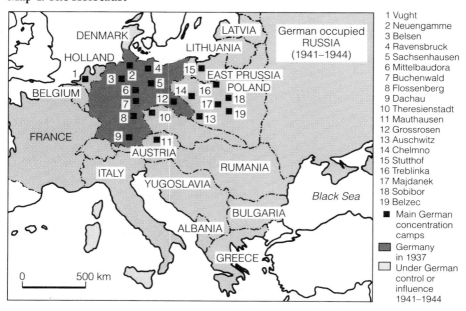